THE HISTORY OF THE WORLD IN FIFTY DOGS

THE HISTORY OF THE WORLD IN FIFTY DOGS

MACKENZI LEE

Illustrations by Petra Eriksson

Abrams Image, New York

Editor: Samantha Weiner
Designer: Danielle Youngsmith
Production Manager: Kathleen Gaffney

Library of Congress Control Number: 2019930872

ISBN: 978-1-4197-4006-0
eISBN: 978-1-68335-763-6

Printed and bound in the United States
10 9 8 7 6 5 4 3 2 1

Abrams Image books are available at special dis-
counts when purchased in quantity for premiums and
promotions as well as fundraising or educational use.
Special editions can also be created to specification.
For details, contact specialsales@abramsbooks.com
or the address below.

Abrams Image® is a registered trademark of Harry
N. Abrams, Inc.

ABRAMS The Art of Books
195 Broadway, New York, NY 10007
abramsbooks.com

**TO ALL THE DOGS I'VE LOVED BEFORE.
BUT ESPECIALLY QUEENIE.**

CONTENTS

PREFACE

As it does for most people, my life completely changed when I got a dog.

I had grown up with dogs, worked as a dog walker, been the fun aunt to all my friends' dogs, leapt out of moving cars to pet random dogs on the street. But it wasn't until I brought home a fourteen-pound fluffy loaf of St. Bernard puppy that I really understood what it means to have a dog.

It means every nice thing you own is going to have teeth marks or slobber or both on it. Or . . . maybe you just don't have nice things anymore. It means you never leave your house not covered in a generous layer of dog hair, and also the amount of time you spend out is determined by how long the pup can hold it. It means a big black nose sometimes shoves its way around the shower curtain when you're in the middle of lathering up. It means reaching down your dog's throat to pry out that dead bird from the gutter they tried to hork down when you weren't looking. It means you wake up at 4:30 A.M. because that now-grown fluff wants to play, which is how you find yourself writing a preface to your book before the sun is up while she delightfully disembowels a stuffed animal at your feet.

It also means that your heart lives outside of your body. It means binding your happiness to that doggy smile and that tail wag. It means wanting to be the person your dog thinks you are, and knowing you never will be, but they will love you anyway. It

means your camera roll fills up with nearly identical photos of your dog sleeping, and you whip them out to show everyone you meet whether they asked for them or not. It means your life is suddenly brimming with a limitless love that runs in two directions.

Turns out, all those clichés about dog ownership are totally true.

As is that age-old adage *write what you know*, which is why, as the past year of my life was completely consumed by my new fluffy dependent who now clocks in at 120 pounds of sass and slobber, I have been compiling stories of dogs in history.

I have loved history since I was young, but I've always found that the pieces that fascinate me the most are not the wars, the politics, the congresses, or the big events people put on plaques. I gravitate toward the quirky, often lesser-known stories that not only prove history was deeply weird, but also show the universalities of the human— and, in this case, canine—experience. These stories of history's dogs provide small windows into the larger historical moments in which they happened and the lives of the humans these animals kept company.

This book contains stories of dogs— real, mythical, and some that are likely a bit of both—but also stories of humans. I have tried not only to tell stories of history's goodest boys, but also to use them to contextualize some pivotal moments from the past. As a self-proclaimed history nerd who slept through her AP Euro class in high school because none of us make good choices when we're sixteen and now has to sheepishly pretend she totally understands the context of the French Revolution, I hope that these small, accessible overviews will provide a foundational knowledge of some crucial historical moments for people who have previously had no idea what was going on.

Depending on where and when they appeared in the timeline, ideas about dogs and their role in society vary hugely. Dogs have been pets, companions, hunters, workers, protectors, pests, experiments; sacred, memorialized, feared, hated, loved, and everything in between. In order to understand dogs, their place in time, and also the particulars of that time *and* place, we are often required to suspend our modern ideas about the dog as pet/meme and, instead, try to look at their stories from the point of view of the world they lived in.

This also requires us to accept that the past is not always kind. In spite of the fact that dogs are perhaps the purest creatures on the earth, not all of these stories are pure, because as good as dogs are, human beings are sometimes the worst. And, as we are wont to do, throughout history we have made dogs complicit in some of our worst moments. I debated whether or not to include these stories in the book, but ultimately chose to do so because I felt they were critical in painting a complete picture both of the role of dogs in history and of history itself. The way we talk about, treat, and remember dogs often tells us more about ourselves than about them.

Now if you'll excuse me, there's a wet nose pressed against my leg, insisting I throw her ball. Enjoy the book.

DOG DOMESTICATION

A Short Introduction to the Notorious D.O.G.

Before we begin this journey through *historius canius*, let's get one big question out of the way: How did dogs go from wild animals to our snuggly pets?

In the discussion of when dogs domesticated, it's important to first make a distinction between domestic and tame. A tame animal is one that becomes accustomed to the presence of people and welcomes human intervention into their lives. Tame animals develop a symbiotic relationship by living closely with people. Domestication, in contrast, happens over generations, and means that an animal lives so closely alongside humans that it becomes dependent upon those humans for survival. Domestication alters animals on both a mental and a physical level. Most domesticated animals that have lived alongside people for multiple generations would not be able to thrive in the wild, due to both learned changes and evolutionary aspects that breed out their ability to fend for themselves. There's a similar difference between wild and feral—wild animals survive their entire lives without human intervention, while feral animals are from a species previously domesticated that has learned to survive on its own.

When we talk about dogs, we're talking about a domesticated animal that can sometimes be feral. When we talk about wolves, it's wild animals that can be tamed.

So. The dogs. When and how did they make the switch from tame wolves to domesticated puppies?

Short answer: We don't know.

Dogs are the most diverse species on earth, besides humans, but every modern dog is related to the wolf. From Chihuahuas to poodles to huskies to corgis, all dog breeds share 99 percent of their DNA with wolves, and since dogs and wolves can still breed with each other, they're considered the same species.

Everyone has a different theory about when dog and wolf broke apart on the evolutionary tree, but it's a pretty impossible question to answer with any certainty, partly because it happened so forking long ago and partly because it probably happened multiple times in multiple places around the world. Wolves and dogs likely diverged sometime between fifteen thousand and forty thousand years ago, which seems like a big range, but it's impressively narrow when we're talking about prehistory.

Some scientists theorize that wolves were domesticated in Europe, others in the Middle East, others in East Asia. To grossly oversimplify things, the dog family tree seems to be separated into two main trunks: dogs from Eastern Eurasia, and dogs from Western Eurasia. The problem is there's evidence supporting the idea that

Eastern dogs migrated west, and other evidence that supports the idea that Western dogs went east. One theory to explain this is that, thousands of years ago, somewhere in western Eurasia, humans domesticated gray wolves. The same thing also happened totally independently in the east. Around the Bronze Age, some of the Eastern dogs migrated westward alongside their human partners, and along the way, these migrants encountered the Western dogs, mated with them, and effectively replaced them.

But. Other scientists think this is totally bogus.

In 2013, a team of scientists compared the mitochondrial genomes (small rings of DNA that sit outside the main set) of 126 modern dogs and wolves and eighteen fossils, and concluded that dogs were domesticated somewhere in Europe or western Siberia. Yet another team compared the full genomes of fifty-eight modern wolves and dogs and concluded that dogs originated in southern China before migrating west.

Obviously, all of these scientists think they're right and the rest are wrong, and obviously there are tons of others, so my brain exploded before I could finish reading about it, because science is Not My Thing.

So where did dogs come from? Who the fork knows?

When? Also, not a clue.

The natural next question, then, is why? Similarly, we don't know.

What can ya do? Science isn't a science.

Some scientists think early human hunter-gatherers actively tamed and bred wolves. A completely different theory is that dogs domesticated themselves—or perhaps there's a dog somewhere writing *The History of the World in Fifty Humans* purporting the theory that dogs domesticated humans. Humans were competitors for food, and so wolves decided if you can't beat them, join them. And the dogs that survived and became most effectively integrated with the humans were the ones with softer fur, brighter eyes, floppier ears, and were generally more adorable—an adorableness that actually has a name: neoteny. Wolf pups who were better at picking up on human social cues, something I still need work on, were more likely to become one of the humans and then breed and make more dogs born into domestication. This theory is (adorably) called Survival of the Friendliest.

Whatever the case, the truth about dog domestication is that we don't really have answers. We don't know for sure how or why or when or where.

What we do know is that whatever act of nature brought us together, dogs and humans have been inseparable ever since.

BARK LIKE AN EGYPTIAN

Abuwtiyuw, History's First Recorded Dog with a Name

TESEM · EGYPT · 16TH CENTURY TO 11TH CENTURY BCE

Before it was an empire known for geometric tombs and kings named Tut, Egypt was a collection of ununified city-states chilling along the Nile. They were divided into two regions—the southern was called the upper kingdom, and the northern was called the lower kingdom. If you're looking at a flat map, it's totally backward, but the kingdoms, like everything else in Egypt, revolved around the flow of the Nile.

If you're planning an ancient empire, the Nile is prime real estate. It was a calm, navigable, and predictable water source, which made trade up and down its four-thousand-mile length super slick. It flooded every year at the same time without the need for irrigation systems, creating ground so fertile that the Egyptians would basically toss seeds like confetti and they'd grow. This left them lots of free time for things like applying eyeliner, inventing papyrus, and doting upon their dogs.

More on that soon—I promise.

Around 3100 BCE, the upper and lower kingdoms united, kicking off the bitchin' empire that we now think of today. Ancient Egypt can be divided into three periods, uncreatively named the Old Kingdom, the Middle Kingdom, and the New Kingdom. Together, these three periods spanned an astonishing thirty centuries, making Egypt one of the greatest hits of ancient world civilizations.

Ancient Egypt is probably best remembered not for what they did in life, but for what they did in death. Structures like the Pyramids of Giza were erected as elaborate tombs built for their pharaohs, who were believed to be literal gods. When a pharaoh died, they were added to the lineup of Egyptian deities and worshiped accordingly, and if someone tells you that after they die they're going to be a god, that's a pretty good reason to give them the best funeral possible. The Egyptians believed that, contrary to the old saying, you *could* take it with you, and so they packed their tombs full of the things that had mattered most to them in life. Things they couldn't live—or rather, die—without.

Which, for some people, was their dog.

When a king, whose name we ironically don't know, lost his beloved dog, he wanted to be sure that the *ka*, or soul, of his dog reached the afterlife and was waiting for him there when his time inevitably came. So he gave the dog a funeral fit for a king and wrote his name in hieroglyphics on the walls of his tomb. Abuwtiyuw, or, as his name is sometimes translated, Abutiu, is one of the earliest known domesticated dogs, and the first in history to have his name recorded. The stone tablet unearthed from the tomb was translated to read, *"The dog which was the guard of His Majesty. Abuwtiyuw is his name. His Majesty ordered that he be buried [ceremonially], that he be given a coffin from the royal treasury, fine linen in great quantity, [and] incense. His Majesty [also] gave perfumed ointment, and [ordered] that a tomb be built for him by the gangs of masons."*

So next time you're meticulously posing your dog for the perfect #dogsofinstagram shot and worry you may be a little extra, remind yourself that at least you aren't employing masons for him. Then post that sh*t because I live for the #dogsofinstagram hashtag.

What breed was Abuwtiyuw? Based on the erect ears and curled tail described on the burial tablet, he was likely what the Egyptians would have called a *tesem*, which was not a breed of dog, but rather the name given to describe all hunting dogs. The actual breed would have resembled the modern Ibizan hound, greyhound, or basenji. His image was also recorded on the walls of his tomb alongside his name.

Abuwtiyuw was one of many mummified dogs that have been unearthed in Egypt, buried both with their owners and in glorious tombs of their own. In the city of Abydos, part of the cemetery was set aside specifically for dogs, and Ashkelon cemetery, in what is today Israel but was once part of Egypt, is the best-preserved dog cemetery of the ancient world. Dogs are depicted in many tomb carvings from across all three periods of Egyptian history, including carvings of men walking their dogs on leashes. Though dog collars and leashes likely date back further than Egypt and originated in Sumeria, it shows that dogs weren't just part of Egyptians' life after death—they were part of their daily lives too.

Egypt may be more commonly associated with cats, but the proof is on the walls: Dogs were found all over the kingdom. While many were used for hunting and protection, that didn't stop them from also being cherished pets like Abuwtiyuw.

Good bois were all over Egypt—it's unde-Nile-able.

shows self out

---

sidebark

Egypt's love for the dog is perhaps best immortalized in the personification of the god Anubis, who is depicted with a jackal head. Egyptians also worshiped the canine deity Wepwawet, a name that means "Opener of Ways." Wepwawet's job was to make a path for the army and to help lead the dead to the underworld. And the god Set was sometimes depicted as a fictional animal called Sha, which looked an awful lot like a dog.

THE XOLOITZCUINTLI

*She Is Beauty, She Is Grace, She Will Lead You to
the Underworld in Spite of Her Weird Face*

XOLOITZCUINTLI · MEXICO · BCE

The Xoloitzcuintli isn't the sort of breed that wins beauty contests. The first thing most people notice about it is that it's completely hairless. Aside from a tufty mohawk of fur on the top of its head, the Xoloitzcuintli is just a bag of wrinkly bluish-black skin. Other prominent features include ears like satellite dishes, a rat tail, and a mouthful of crooked, missing teeth.

But take another look.

Okay, maybe one more look. And squint a little this time. And ignore the fact that they are often mistaken as chupacabras, the mythical creature at the very top of the list of "Mythical Creatures You Hope No One Ever Mistakes You For."

I promise, they have a great personality.

Even though they're perhaps not the most, shall we say, conventionally attractive dogs on the planet, Xoloitzcuintlis have a long, storied past and are remembered as some of the first domesticated dogs of North America.

First, let's get this out of the way: It's pronounced show-low-eats-QUEENT-lee. Or you can call them Xolo, or show-lo for short. The Xolo gets its name from two words in the language of the Aztecs: Xolotl, the god of lightning and death, and *itzcuintli*, which means *dog*.

The Xolo was a sacred dog to many of the indigenous people of the Americas, including the Colima, Mayans, Toltec, Zapotec, and Aztec. Some researchers believe that the Xolo accompanied the earliest migrants from Asia over three thousand years ago. The Xolo's trademark hairlessness, which some, like this author, may think is super weird and upsetting and kind of makes them look like balls, was the result of an ancient genetic mutation, but ended up being a beneficial trait, as it helped them survive in the tropical climates of Central America. The same mutation also gives many of them a horrific dental situation. But— silver lining!—their distinct teeth—or rather, lack of teeth—makes it easy for archaeologists to identify their remains when they're uncovered.

According to Aztec mythology, the god Xolotl made the Xoloitzcuintli from a sliver of the Bone of Life from which all mankind was made. Xolotl gave this gift to man with the instruction to guard and protect it. In exchange, the Xolo would guide the Aztecs through the dangers of Mictlan, the underworld. Effigies of Xolo were often placed in tombs to represent this shepherding to the next life. In some Mexican states, almost 75 percent of all ancient graves contained some kind of Xolo vessel. Unfortunately, that job as the first guide dog usually involved being sacrificed in order to accompany their dead people. Even worse—the Xolo were occasionally eaten as delicacies for ceremonies like marriages and funerals. Moving on.

XOLO GETS ITS NAME FROM TWO WORDS IN THE LANGUAGE OF THE AZTECS: XOLOTL, THE GOD OF LIGHTNING AND DEATH, AND *ITZCUINTLI*, WHICH MEANS *DOG*.

Aside from their afterlife responsibilities, Aztecs believed the Xolo had healing powers—and they were actually kind of right. If you've ever woken in the middle of the night overheated because your dog has decided to lie on top of you, you know how warm dogs can get. And since they have no hair, Xolos are basically canine hot water bottles. They were often placed in beds with the sick to help regulate body temperatures, which helped with the healing process. Their snuggling was legendary and revered.

These hairless weirdos were first documented for European audiences by the sixteenth-century Spanish missionary Bernardino de Sahagún, who describes how the Aztecs would wrap their Xolos in blankets each night to keep them warm. They also caught the eye of Christopher Columbus, and because he couldn't keep his hands to himself, he ended up taking several Xolos back to Europe with him (he and his men also nearly ate them into extinction, because he just couldn't get enough of genocide. Christopher Columbus was *not* a good boy).

But in spite of their legendary past, and later in history having famous owners like Diego Rivera and Frida Kahlo, the Xolo very nearly died out in the twentieth century. It was thanks to the indigenous culture revival in Mexico (an effort to preserve culture that was lost when the Europeans came in and smashed everything), as well as some key appearances by Xolo in popular culture (you may remember Dante, the *bueno perro* in the Pixar movie *Coco*? He's a Xolo!), the Xolo became an official AKC breed in 2011.

Who says looks are everything?

PANHU MAKES FETCH HAPPEN

Chinese Mythology's Original Ancestor

CHINA

Dogs are an important part of the mythology and lore of cultures across the world. From Hades's hound, Cerberus, to Ireland's Inis Fáil, a dog who never failed to catch its prey and also turned any water he bathed in to wine, which is #goals, to Amaguq, the Inuit trickster wolf god. To tell all those stories would be another book entirely.

So let's just talk about one—the story of Panhu, one of the most fascinating dogs from folklore I found while researching this book. This story is widely known in South China, and some indigenous groups, including Miao, Yao, and She, consider Panhu their original ancestor.

As with most myths, there are a lot of variations of the story. But Panhu's origins are always beautifully weird: Once upon a time, an old woman in Emperor Ku's palace thought she suffered from ringing in the ears, but when she consulted a doctor, he removed a bug from her ear and the ringing stopped. The old woman put the bug in a gourd and covered it with a tray to keep as a pet, which is something my mom would 100 percent do. Through some mythological magic, the bug became a five-colored dog that the Emperor Ku named Panhu—*hu*

meaning "gourd" and *pan* meaning "tray." Which, if I were a god dog, Gourd Tray would not be my first choice of name, but you do you, Gourd Tray.

Emperor Ku's reign was defined by conflict with barbarian invaders, led by a nefarious evil general whom some accounts refer to as General Wu. Emperor Ku got tired of losing to General Wu, so he issued an order that whoever brought him the head of General Wu would receive his daughter's hand in marriage.

Not long after, Panhu appeared in the court with the head of General Wu in his mouth.

He had, like any good dog, fetched.

To which Emperor Ku said, "I've made a huge mistake."

For obvious reasons, he was not excited about marrying his daughter to a dog. But the princess made a case for the importance of the emperor keeping his word, and convinced her father to let her marry Panhu. Which, relatable, because TBH, a dog to have and to hold in sickness and in health till death do us part is my actual dream. But it does present some logistical issues in the areas of, shall we say, marital intimacy.

Particularly if you're looking for the princess and her betrothed to produce heirs to your kingdom.

But then—magic arrives to save the day! The emperor was told that Panhu could be transformed into a human by being placed beneath a large gold bell for seven days and seven nights, but the spell would only work if no one looked upon him for the entirety of those seven days. But the princess became concerned for her dog/husband/things are confusing, and on the sixth day, she peeked under the bell. The spell was broken and Panhu's transfiguration halted. He had the body of a man, but his head was still all dog.

And the princess was like, "That works." And, reader, she married him.

The Yao people honor Panhu as their first ancestor, and as a result, they are very careful not to offend dogs. They also will not eat dog meat—let's talk about this for a second.

In some ethnic groups in China, as well as other Asian countries, dog meat has been a source of food from around 500 BCE. Some scientists believe dogs were first domesticated in China to serve as a food source. Today, the consumption of dog meat in China varies by region, as do attitudes about it. In Hong Kong, the Dogs and Cats Ordinance was introduced by the British Hong Kong government on January 6, 1950. It prohibits the slaughter of any dog or cat for use as food. Taiwan, India, and Singapore all have similar bans. However, certain cultural food festivals continue to serve it.

THE YAO PEOPLE HONOR PANHU AS THEIR FIRST ANCESTOR, AND AS A RESULT, THEY ARE VERY CAREFUL NOT TO OFFEND DOGS.

So yeah, it's a thing that happens. And much like all things that happen, it's complicated, and a lot of people have a lot of thoughts on it.

Aside from the taboo against eating dog meat in certain regions, the story of Panhu is still an important part of life for many ethnic groups in southern China. Many have altars to dogs in their homes, and iconography associated with Panhu is used in traditional clothing.

ARGOS, THE LOYAL DOG OF THE *ODYSSEY*

Western Literature's First Dead Dog

GREECE · 750 BCE

The *Iliad* and the *Odyssey* are the two oldest pieces of Western literature, written sometime around the eighth century. Though their authorship continues to be debated—some scholars believe it was the sole work of Homer, others that it was a collaboration among many authors. Whatever the case, Homer wasn't the first person to tell the story. The stories of Odysseus and the Trojan War had been passed down through the oral tradition for generations before Homer put pen to paper. Or quill to papyrus. Or chisel to stone—however he wrote it down. You get the point.

The *Iliad* is set during the Trojan War, the ten-year siege of the city of Troy, which may or may not be fictional, and, according to what Hollywood taught me, no one wore an appropriate amount of clothes for war, and everyone was very fit and oiled. According to legends, the Trojan War began when King Menelaus's wife was stolen by the Trojan prince Paris. Menelaus responded by launching a thousand ships, which he may have intended to be a grand romantic gesture, but it came off as a gesture of war, which the *Iliad* chronicles. Not only is the *Iliad* the first epic piece of Western literature,

it was so lit it spawned a second part—*Iliad 2: Tokyo Drift*. No, just kidding—that was definitely not the title, but even back in the eighth century, popular demand was a thing, and Homer soon put out the *Odyssey*, a sequel that would go down in history as one of the great sequels, alongside *The Empire Strikes Back* and *Toy Story 2*. The *Odyssey* puts one of the *Iliad*'s minor characters, Odysseus, king of the Greek kingdom of Ithaca, center stage and documents his incredibly involved journey home. According to the *Odyssey*, it took him two years in spite of the fact that it's really not that far, because he is constantly distracted by everything, from a cyclops to sea nymphs. When Odysseus finally makes it home, it's to find that everyone thinks he's dead (because why wouldn't they when he took so damn long to travel like two blocks?), his palace has been trashed, and random dudes are making the moves on his wife, Penelope, who, in spite of everything, is still waiting for his return. In order to gain access to his own palace and take his place again on the throne, Odysseus has to disguise himself as a beggar.

Here's where the dog comes in. Before he left, Odysseus had a dog named Argos.

This is how you know this is a fictional text: because one, he didn't take his dog with him, and two, when he comes back twenty years later, his dog is still alive somehow. But I get it—it's a literary device meant to tug at our heartstrings.

As Odysseus approaches his home, he finds Argos, his once fast and sleek hunting dog, lying neglected on a pile of cow manure, his coat infested with fleas and lice. Unlike everyone else in his home, Argos recognizes Odysseus at once, in spite of his disguise, and wags his tail. But Odysseus can't go to Argos without betraying who he actually is, so he is forced to walk by Argos and into the palace without having a viral video–worthy reunion with his dog after so many years apart. Which breaks. My. Heart.

But don't worry—it gets worse. Argos, having finally seen his master at last, or perhaps bereft over the fact that his master ignored him, can finally move on. He dies, the first in a long line of dog deaths in Western literature meant to evoke emotion, and boy, do they get me every time.

The *Iliad* and the *Odyssey* are still read, and for good reason. Though there's some debate whether the Trojan War

UNLIKE EVERYONE ELSE IN HIS HOME, ARGOS RECOGNIZES ODYSSEUS AT ONCE, IN SPITE OF HIS DISGUISE, AND WAGS HIS TAIL.

actually happened, what matters isn't so much whether it did or didn't. We know that a war did take place around a city that was most likely Troy and it was destroyed, but whether fictional or not, it became a defining moment in Greek cultural identity, because it was the first time the Greek kingdoms came together in unification. The Ancient Greeks were obsessed with the events of that great war and told the stories over and over again. And as the Greek idea of cultural identity changed over time, so did their stories. The Greeks all gained their collective identity from the Trojan War, and that identity was personified in Homer's epic poems.

No single text has provided more insight into the lives of the Ancient Greeks than the *Iliad*. And no dog proved so loyal as little old Argos.

---

sidebark

The term "dog days" originated with the Greeks. They used it to refer to the days when Sirius, the dog star, appeared to rise before the sun, which was in late July. These days were the hottest time of the year.

ALL DOGS GO TO HEAVEN

King Yudhisthira and the Dog of the Mahābhārata

MUTT · INDIA · 3RD CENTURY BCE

The Mahābhārata is one of the two major Sanskrit epics from Ancient India. It tells the story of the Kurukṣhetra War, which mostly involved two families fighting for the throne of the kingdom of Hastinapura—the Kauravas and the Pandavas—and then an internal struggle within each family about who is the rightful heir. I have a theory that every culture and every age has an equivalent of *Game of Thrones*, and this was Ancient India's.

But let's skip ahead to the dog.

The Mahābhārata ends with a series of battles on the field of Kurukshetra. All the Kauravas are killed, and, though the Pandavas are victorious, only five brothers survive. Yudhisthir, the oldest of the brothers, becomes king, and rules for thirty years before he and his brothers make a pilgrimage to their final resting place in the Himalayas. Along the journey, each of the brothers and their wives died, until only Yudhisthira was left.

Yudhisthira and, more important, a dog.

At the beginning of their journey, a stray dog had begun to follow his company, and it made the last leg of the ascent at Yudhisthira's side.

At last, when they reached the summit of the mountain, Indra, the king of the gods and king of heaven, ascended in his chariot to meet King Yudhisthira and invited him to come to heaven.

"Sure," said King Yudhisthira. "So long as the dog comes too."

But Indra didn't seem to understand that all dogs go to heaven, and refused entry.

To which King Yudhisthira replied, "K, bye."

He refused to enter without his dog. The pleasures of heaven couldn't compare to the loss of his faithful companion who had traveled his whole journey with him.

And, TBH, same. If there aren't dogs in heaven, I don't want to go there. Honestly, anywhere there aren't dogs is not somewhere I want to be.

But then Indra pulled an old switcheroo.

Turns out, the dog was actually the deity Yama in disguise (is this where the palindromic god and dog came from? We may never know). The whole thing was a final test for Yudhisthira, and Indra probably laughed and said, "Did you seriously think dogs couldn't get into heaven? They are the goodest, purest, best bois."

THE PLEASURES OF HEAVEN COULDN'T COMPARE TO THE LOSS OF HIS FAITHFUL COMPANION WHO HAD TRAVELED HIS WHOLE JOURNEY WITH HIM.

The *Mahābhārata* is an important source of information on the development of Hinduism. Hindus regard it as both a text about dharma, which is Hindu moral law, and history. The poem covers a wide range of myths and legends—so much that the actual plot of the feuding families is only about one-fifth of the one hundred thousand couplets that comprise it. It contains about 1.8 million words and has been called the longest poem ever written. Cool, cool, cool, cool—that sounds like my nightmare, but cool, cool.

The *Mahābhārata* story has been told and retold throughout South and Southeast Asia for centuries. Elements of and stories from the poem have inspired everything from modern TV shows to the sculptured reliefs at Angkor Wat in Cambodia.

And, most important, the story definitively cleared the path for thousands of good dogs to cross the rainbow bridge into dog heaven.

PERITAS THE GREAT

The Somewhat Mythical Dog of Alexander the Great

MOLOSSUS (MASTIFF) · MESOPOTAMIA · 336–323 BCE

Long before he was great, Alexander was born in 356 BCE to the Macedonian king Philip II and one of his wives, Olympias (according to some legends, Alexander was actually the result of a union between Olympias and a snake that was a god). At the time, Macedonia was a kingdom in the northeastern corner of the Greek peninsula and was considered a brutal and uncivilized place, particularly in comparison to nearby Athens and Sparta. So when Philip brought in Aristotle to serve as a teacher to young Alexander, it was the equivalent of bringing Stephen Hawking in to tutor the cast of *Jersey Shore*. But Philip was a brilliant military mind who was working to conquer Greece and wanted his son to someday take his place, which required the best teaching available. After his son had tamed an untamable horse at the age of thirteen, Philip was certain his heir was destined to be . . . well, great.

While Alexander was learning at the knee of the most famous philosopher of all time, his dad was slowly and surely conquering Greece, which was not in great shape. Their navy had become weak, and the primary focus of the people had shifted from the military to culture, which is great, but you don't win wars with a poem, unless that poem is very pointy. Greece was the ancient empire equivalent of being passed out, wasted on a couch at a frat party, begging to have its forehead drawn on. And Alexander's father, Philip, was the one to wield the Sharpie.

At the tender age of eighteen, Alexander assisted his father in completing his invasion of Greece, which inspired in Alexander a lifelong passion for conquering. After Philip died, Alexander took the Macedonian throne and picked up his father's legacy of bursting into places he was not invited, calling them his, and killing anyone who got in his way. Over the next decade, he expanded his empire through the great strategy of never losing a battle. His father had conquered all of Greece, but Alexander broke up the Persian empire and claimed land from Egypt to India.

Though none of that would have possible without the intervention of his dog, Peritas.

Though his breed wasn't recorded, based on artistic renderings, Peritas was most likely a molossus, a dog bred for fighting in war. Though now extinct, they resembled mastiffs and are an important common ancestor of modern breeds like the English mastiff, St. Bernard, Great Pyrenees, rottweiler, Great Dane, Newfoundland, and Bernese mountain dog.

Peritas distinguished himself during the Battle of Gaugamela against the Persians. During the fight, Alexander found himself cut off from his men when a war elephant charged at him, but Peritas, who had been his companion on the campaign, leapt (probably in slow motion, possibly from a helicopter) in front of his hooman. He grabbed the elephant by the lip and hung on tight, which resulted in enough blood loss to weaken the elephant and give Alexander and Peritas time to escape.

The story sound ridiculous, and probably isn't true—Plutarch, the only ancient historian to mention Peritas by name, only says that Alexander had a dog named Peritas that he loved so much he named a city after him. On the other hand, remember molossuses were bred to fight wars, and armies at that time often used elephants and lions in battle, so a dog on the battlefield would have to be prepared to face wild animals.

Also, Alexander's mom supposedly slept with a god snake. So. Take it all with one enormous grain of salt.

By saving Alexander's life, Peritas made it possible for him to take Persia, a previously unachievable feat that cemented his reputation as a badass and paved the way for his conquering of everywhere else. Throughout his empire, Alexander would either rechristen existing cities or establish new ones all named after himself (most called Alexandra, but he also threw an Alexandropolis in there, which I can't read without giggling).

But he proclaimed one conquered city to be named after Peritas, and put a monument to his dog in the central square as thanks for saving his life in battle.

Alexander was great at making empires. Not great at maintaining them. After he smashed a city to pieces, he wasn't interested in investing much time in building it back up again. Which is why, when he died in 323 BCE, his empire was immediately split into three, each known as the Hellenistic kingdoms, and each ruled by one of his generals. All of these three kingdoms lasted longer than Alexander's empire.

Whether Alexander was actually as great as history remembers him—both in terms of the brilliance of his military mind and the actual greatness of what he was doing, because conquering empires usually involves a fair amount of genocide—is up for debate. But his impact on the world was undeniable. He introduced the idea of absolute monarchy to the Greco-Roman world. He gave the region a common language—Greek—which facilitated trade. His reach was so vast that modern archaeologists have found coins in Afghanistan written in Greek. He founded twenty cities and was a role model for other questionable conquerors like Julius Caesar and Napoleon. Alexander didn't make those things happen, but they wouldn't have happened without him.

And none of it would have happened without the intervention of Peritas the dog.

IMPERIAL CHINA'S ADORABLE MACE

The Pekingese and Other Lion Dogs of China

PEKINGESE · CHINA · 220–280

The Pekingese have been around since the Shu dynasty in China, two thousand years ago, making them one of the oldest dog breeds still in existence today. Shu, or Shu Han, was one of the three major states that competed for supremacy over China between 220 and 280, which is fittingly known as the Three Kingdoms period. In spite of the "kingdom" part of that title, none of these states were ruled by kings—instead they were governed by emperors, each of whom thought they controlled all of China.

During this time, China became a Buddhist country, but this conversion faced a significant stumbling block: The lion, which was an important symbol in Buddhism, didn't live in China. It was believed that Buddha had tamed the lion and made it his protector, so the lion was necessary for many religious ceremonies.

Since there were no lions handy, the Buddhist monks decided to improvise.

They used dogs.

sticks wig on a dog; posts to Instagram

In order to make the dog a suitable stand-in for Buddha's lion, the monks undertook a program of selective breeding. At first, dogs were bred for size and fuzziness in order to most resemble the lion. Over the course of several centuries, they scaled down until they had created a small dog that looked enough like a little lion that the monks felt Buddha wouldn't mind if it was used in religious ceremonies instead of an actual lion. They called this dog the Pekingese.

THE PEKINGESE HAVE BEEN AROUND SINCE THE SHU DYNASTY IN CHINA, TWO THOUSAND YEARS AGO, MAKING THEM ONE OF THE OLDEST DOG BREEDS STILL IN EXISTENCE TODAY.

The Pekingese became a sacred symbol in Chinese Buddhism, but they were too adorable to be purely ceremonial, and were soon kept as pets by the imperial court. And *only* the imperial court. Common people were forbidden from owning or breeding the Pekingese, and had to bow down to any Pekingese they saw. The penalty for being cruel to a Pekingese or removing one from the royal palace was death.

The smallest and most ferocious variety was known as the sleeve Pekingese because emperors and courtiers took to carrying the dogs in their voluminous sleeves. If the owners felt threatened or found themselves on the wrong end of an assassination attempt, they'd unleash the Pekingese from their sleeve upon the attacker, effectively scaring him off (and probably also scarring him). It was the Ancient Chinese equivalent of pepper spray—in the words of the Internet, he protec but he also attac.

The Pekingese remained a purely Chinese breed until 1860. The summer palace in Beijing was stormed by English troops in the Second Opium War, a conflict between China and the British Empire over who got to own China—which, unsurprisingly, England did not think should be China—as well as the British opium trade. Basically, the continuing saga of White People Being the Worst. To keep their sacred dogs from falling into invading hands, the Chinese royal family killed their dogs. But five Pekingese survived and were brought back to England. One was given to Queen Victoria, who was already a dog lover. The arrival of the Pekingese kicked off the newest fashion craze in Victorian England: lapdogs. Owning a lapdog quickly became the ultimate status symbol, as well as a way to show off the fact that you not only had enough money to feed your family, you could also feed a completely decorative dog that served no working purpose other than cuteness and cuddles.

As a result of the Industrial Revolution, a newly moneyed middle class had emerged in Europe, and they had time on their hands they didn't know what to do with. As a result, breeding dogs and keeping them as pets, or the "dog fancy," as it was known, quickly became the hobby of choice. Though most did not have access to the pure, rare Pekingese, many were able to produce their own knockoff version of the elite's essential canine accessory. This attempt to create similar-looking lapdogs jump-started the creation of many of the toy breeds we still pet today.

Though most of us don't have the sleeves to hold them.

sidebark

🐕 The Pekingese ("Peke"), the Lhasa apso, and the Tibetan mastiff were all bred in China to resemble lions for Buddhism. In addition, the pug and shih tzu also originated at this time as companions and protection for the imperial court, though they were too snub-nosed and flat-faced to conceivably pass as lions.

🐕 Emperor Ling of Han, who ruled from 168 to 189, loved his dogs so much he made his favorite Pekingese a member of the noble caste, which meant it outranked most people in the country. All hail.

THE DOG KING OF NORWAY HAS NO IDEA WHAT HE'S DOING

Scandinavia's Mythical History of Ruff Regents

NORWEGIAN ELKHOUND · SCANDANAVIA · 6TH CENTURY

No, it's not a pitch for a new Disney movie—though there's nothing in the rules that says a dog *can't* be king. The dog king is a legendary part of Scandinavian mythology, and many versions of it appear across regional folklore. The most famous of these myths, which is often presented as historical fact even though it's fairly unlikely that it was true, comes from Norway.

The story starts with King Eystein the Bad, a name that gets right to the point. Eystein the Unsubtle was king of the Norwegian Uplands, and when his forces conquered the city of Trondheim, one of Norway's main hubs, he played the benevolent father and installed his son as king. The people of Trondheim were not crazy about being conquered, and less about having an invader's son now making the rules, so they did what any disgruntled population would do: They rose up and murdered him. Eystein the Furious managed to subdue this uprising and reclaim Trondheim, but as punishment for their insubordination, he gave the people a choice: As a replacement for his son, he would either install his slave on the throne or install his dog. (This was meant to be the ultimate humiliation, because, wow, people are really good at dehumanizing others by comparing them to animals.)

The people chose the dog, probably because they assumed he'd be easier to get rid of.

Smash cut to three years later, and His Royal Majesty King Saur—who, remember, is a dog—was still on the throne. And Saur translates from Icelandic to . . . Since my mom is going to read this book, let's say it means "poop." Eystein the Petty put his dog named King Poop on the throne.

In the account of King Saur's reign by the Icelandic poet Snorri Sturluson (which, BTW, is an awesome name for a dog, or possibly a gnome prince), Saur was said to possess "three men's wisdom," and he was able to speak one word for every two woofs (obviously, this is the part of the story where we start to lean heavily on legend). Sturluson wrote that Saur had his own set of regal robes (undoubtedly with a little hole for his tail) and gold and silver chains to wear around his neck, and his courtiers carried him on their shoulders "when the weather or ways were foul." And while I can't find any evidence that he had a tiny crown, if he didn't, I'll retroactively make him one because there's nothing quite as adorable as a big dog in a tiny hat. Like any self-respecting despot, King Saur also had a throne, and a palace on an island that became known as Saurshoug. Which translates to (hi, Mom!) "poop pile." Whether or not the dog king was real, Saurshoug definitely was—Sturluson noted that the name was still used for the area in his day, centuries later.

King Saur met his end when wolves broke into the royal cow pen and he ran to defend his bovine subjects, but the legend lived on. In addition to Sturluson's writings, Saur also appears in *The Heimskringla*, a collection of sagas of the Norwegian kings,

SAUR WAS SAID TO POSSESS "THREE MEN'S WISDOM," AND HE WAS ABLE TO SPEAK ONE WORD FOR EVERY TWO WOOFS.

as well as several other stories of semimythical historical tales of Norwegian and Swedish history. The Danes have their own story of a canine monarch. His name is Rakke, which is the Old Danish word for "dog," and he was appointed to rule over the Danes by the Swedish king Adils in a similar attempt to humiliate his conquered subjects. His story also ends with him running to defend his cattle from wolves and losing the fight.

Gives a whole new meaning to the phrase "dogs rule," doesn't it?

---

sidebark

 Though we don't know for sure what breed these dog kings were, the most famous breed from Scandinavia is the Norwegian elkhound. Similar to the Akita or Alaskan malamute in appearance, the Norwegian elkhound came from the land of ice and snow around 5000 BCE, and still exists today with all its Nordic traits intact. The elkhound appears in epic sagas of ancient times, and many were buried alongside their Viking masters. Elkhounds were both companions on board the Vikings' ships, and hunters on land. They specialized in following the scent trail of their prey (sometimes elk, but also badgers, lynx, reindeer, bears, wolves, and rabbits) over long distances and holding them at bay until the trailing huntsmen arrived. Elkhounds look nothing like the droopy-eared, sleek-coated scent hounds we think of as hunting dogs today, but they are classified as hounds because of this job description.

In times of war, the Norwegian defense minister has the authority to mobilize all privately owned Norwegian elkhounds for the protection of the country.

ST. ROCH, THE PATRON SAINT OF DOGS

Lord, Make Me an Instrument of Thy Treats

EUROPE · 1300s

Our accounts of the life of St. Roch, like the lives of most of the Catholic saints, are a blend of myth, faith, symbolism, and fact. It's hard to separate them.

But no matter how large a grain of salt you take this story with, St. Roch is an important figure to Catholics and dog lovers alike— after all, he is the patron saint of dogs.

St. Roch lived from around 1295 to 1327, and his work stretched over France, Spain, and Italy. He was born in Montpellier, France, with a birthmark on his chest in the shape of a cross, which is a pretty unsubtle sign that he was destined for holy things. But when he was twenty and his parents died, he still hadn't done anything particularly saintly. Fearing that his parents' deaths had been God's punishment for not taking up the work prophesied by his birthmark (BRB—checking myself for any birthmarks in the shape of me dating Tom Hiddleston), he turned over all his inherited land and money to the poor. He even gave up the governorship of Montpellier, which his father had granted to him on his deathbed (his parents were rich, in case that wasn't clear), and set off on a pilgrimage to Rome.

The only thing he took with him was the family dog.

Roch arrived in Italy during an outbreak of the plague. As he passed through the towns of Acquapendente, Cesena, Rimini, and Novara, he observed hundreds of sick people with open sores that caused them debilitating pain, many of whom were turned out onto the streets or quarantined to small, poorly maintained sections of the city. Like everyone else, Roch was afraid to get too close for fear of contracting the plague himself.

But his dog had different ideas. Roch noticed that, when they passed plague victims, his dog would lick the sores on their skin. The healing power of a dog wasn't a new superstition. In Ancient Egypt, the city of Hardai used dogs in medicine, which contributed to its nickname, City of Dogs. Many Egyptians believed that being licked by a dog sped the healing process. At the Temple of Asclepius, the Ancient Greeks employed sacred dogs to lick the wounds of sick petitioners. Today we know that a dog's saliva *can* help clean a wound—it will loosen any debris that may be on the surface and contains simple proteins called histatins that can help ward off infections and close a wound. So, shockingly, history got it right.

Roch was inspired by his dog's ministrations and decided to follow his example. As weird and awesome as it would be to have a saint who went around licking plague victims, St. Roch took the spirit of his pup rather than the letter for inspiration: He began tracing the sign of the cross with his finger onto the bodies of plague victims while praying over them. He *touched* plague victims! With his *finger*! And then he probably touched a bunch of other stuff, like doorknobs and light switches and his iPhone, and got plague germs everywhere even though he didn't have either of those last two things and no one knew what germs were!

Miraculously—literally, this was his first saintly miracle—the sores of these plague victims began to heal. Though whether it was actually godly or just Roch taking credit for science is up for debate. In every city he visited on his way to Rome, Roch and his dog offered the sick touch, prayers, and puppy kisses.

But, as miraculous as his healing powers were, they didn't keep him from the effects of what usually happens when you spend a lot of time touching people with infectious diseases: You also get sick. Roch soon developed the plague himself, and withdrew to the forests surrounding Rome. He made himself a little hut and settled down, presumably to either die slowly or heal miraculously. His dog, of course, went with him. While Roch was sleeping off the plague (that's a thing, right?), his dog got to work saving his life.

The dog found a castle nearby that belonged to an aristocrat named Gothard.

People were gathered for a feast in the dining hall when suddenly a dog appeared, put his paws up on the table, and helped himself to a loaf of bread. Unlike every other dog in history, he didn't eat what he took from the table—instead, he carried it in his mouth. Gothard was amused, then shocked when this canine Jean Valjean kept coming back day after day, stealing a loaf of bread, and leaving without eating it. Finally, Gothard followed him back to Roch's hut in the forest, where he watched the dog drop the food on the lap of his master, then lie down at his side and lick his plague sores.

Gothard was so moved that he took up the care of St. Roch, who eventually recovered without any scars—another sign of his saintliness. When Roch thanked God for preserving him, his prayers included thanks for his dog.

Roch eventually returned home to Montpellier, but France was neck-deep in civil war, and he was mistaken for a spy. Both Roch and his dog were imprisoned for five years, until Roch's death. While in prison, he continued to share the word of God and minister to the other prisoners.

Today, Roch is remembered by Catholics as the patron saint of many things—bachelors, surgeons, people who have been falsely accused of crimes, but, most important, dogs. Though neither the dog's name nor his breed were preserved, in most depictions of St. Roch, he's accompanied by a faithful little mutt, often licking his wounds or carrying a loaf of bread in his mouth.

If I'm to be remembered, let me always be depicted with a dog.

DONCHADH, ROBERT THE BRUCE'S LOYAL HOUND

Unintentionally Becomes Dog the Bounty Hunter

BLOODHOUND · SCOTLAND · 1300s

It's hard to get along with your neighbors. Especially when one of those neighbors claims all your land and makes you swear loyalty to their king and pay taxes to them.

Which is why England and Scotland have had a rather rocky relationship.

Since 1066, Scotland and England each had their own king, but England's king was the supreme king, and the Scottish kings were required to pledge that they would do whatever England wanted. Part of this oath of fealty was that Scotland couldn't appoint a new king without England's approval, which was a problem when King Alexander III died with no heir. King Edward I of England stepped in to pick from the two claimants to the throne, and he selected John Balliol, after John acknowledged him as his rightful lord.

With his puppet on the throne, Edward demanded Scotland help him finance and provide troops for England's current war with France. In response, the Scottish government decided to pull a double cross and signed a treaty of alliance with France, and King John renounced his fealty to the English. Edward was, shall we say, upset. Upset enough to invade Scotland.

After several crushing defeats, the Scottish army collapsed. King John abdicated, and Edward took over running Scotland, claiming all lands were his.

But the long arm of the law can only stretch so far, and the north of Scotland is a long way from England, and also it's really cold and there are lots of mountains, so the English control of those territories was weak, making them the perfect place for a rebellion to begin. The efforts of the rebels were eventually enough to push England back out of Scotland and William Wallace, leader of the rebels in central Scotland, was appointed guardian of the realm.

Edward was, to put it mildly, enraged. You can probably guess what happens next. REINVASION.

William Wallace was captured and executed. England had its fingers back in Scotland and declared it an official territory. Scotland was still pretty sure it belonged to itself. Two new rivals for the Scottish throne emerged—Robert the Bruce and John Comyn. They did not like each other. But then Robert found a clever and a simple way to get rid of Comyn's claim: He murdered him.

In 1306, Robert the Bruce was crowned king of Scotland and began focusing on recovering the southern Scottish lands, which were still held by the English. In the eyes of Edward, this was treason, and he sent his men to hunt down Robert the Bruce.

Robert's wife's company had already been captured by the British, and that company included his favorite dog, Donnchadh. Donnchadh was a Talbot (an early ancestor of the modern bloodhound), and his name is pronounced DON-nu-chu. It's an old Gaelic name that smooshed together the words for "brown" and "noble," which is an appropriate name for dogs for a few reasons. This name would eventually evolve into the name Duncan.

When Edward's chief minion, John of Loren, was tasked with finding Robert, he came up with a brilliant plan to use the dog. John ordered his men to set the dog free, believing Donnchadh would lead them straight to Robert.

And, because he was a dog and thus had only a 20 percent understanding of what was going on, Donnchadh immediately picked up his master's scent and took off, leading the English soldiers directly to where Robert and his men were hiding.

However, one thing went wrong with this brilliant English plot: A dog that's loyal enough to find his master is also loyal enough to fight for him.

When the soldiers surrounded Robert, Donnchadh turned on them and attacked. Robert and his dog both escaped the ambush, and the Bruce continued to lead his guerilla warfare against the English.

Eventually, the two armies met at the Battle of Bannockburn, and though the English by all means should have won, they didn't.

By this time, Edward had died, and his son Edward II (because all kings must be named the same thing to make history as confusing as possible), took over. He was more "meh" about war with Scotland, mostly because his own nobles were on the brink of civil war and he was dealing with that domestic crisis. Which is likely why the English didn't bring the A game to Bannockburn.

WHEN THE SOLDIERS SURROUNDED ROBERT, DONNCHADH TURNED ON THEM AND ATTACKED. ROBERT AND HIS DOG BOTH ESCAPED THE AMBUSH, AND THE BRUCE CONTINUED TO LEAD HIS GUERILLA WARFARE AGAINST THE ENGLISH.

In 1320, Scottish nobles sent the Declaration of Arbroath to the Pope. It stated that Scotland was an independent kingdom, Robert was the true king, and the English could suck it.

After another unsuccessful attempt by England to take over Scotland, the two sides signed the Treaty of Edinburgh–Northampton, which stated that Scotland was its own kingdom and the Bruces were the rightful heirs of the Scottish throne and settled the border as exactly what it was before the war.

Obviously, this didn't last. Scotland and England continued to go toe to toe for many years before the Acts of Union of

1707, which united the two. But the Bruce's claim to the throne had even greater ramifications for the birth of a completely different nation. Robert ultimately married his daughter into the House of Stuart, a noble line that came to rule England. One of the most famous members of this family, and a direct descendant of Robert the Bruce, is none other than King George III, who, during his reign, managed to antagonize a bunch of nobodies until they launched a revolution against his rule in their thirteen colonies on the other side of the Atlantic.

But we all know that story already.

---

sidebark

 Bloodhounds as we know them were brought from Constantinople and perfected in Western Europe about a thousand years ago. Many churches kept packs of hounds on the grounds of the monasteries of England and France, funded by noble lords. The monks were charged with the breeding program and making sure that the lords' hounds only bred with other lords' hounds. Their hounds came to be known as "blooded hounds"—"blooded" meaning "of aristocratic blood."

Police departments around the world rely on bloodhounds' incredible ability to track by scent. Testimony of a bloodhound's trail is admissible in almost every court.

The bloodhound's loose skin and long ears aren't just adorably droopy—they're used to waft scents more effectively toward their nose. The flap of skin beneath their throat is called dewlap, and you can find it on other breeds, like St. Bernards, mastiffs, and basset hounds. They're most commonly seen in dogs from colder climates because the loose skin provides a layer of fat that protects the trachea in extremely cold air. It helps warm the air the dog is breathing to an above-freezing temperature before it gets to the lungs and damages the tissue.

CONQUISTADOGS!

In Which Dogs Are Forced to Be Complicit in Colonialism

MOLOSSUS (MASTIFF) · AMERICA · 1400–1500

There's a reason Shakespeare wrote "let slip the dogs of war." Dogs have been unwitting tools of battle throughout history (remember Peritas, who you just read about? And if you skipped that entry, go back and read it because it's awesome). In Europe, during the Middle Ages and Renaissance, there was rarely a battlefield without a legion of dog soldiers on it. A letter from Queen Elizabeth I's reign states that three hundred mastiffs were used against the Irish, and King Henry VIII was said to have sent hundreds of war dogs to the Emperor Charles V of Spain to aid him in a war with France.

So the conquistadors who laid claim to the already-claimed Americas were part of a long legacy of using dogs to fight their battles.

It's difficult to discuss the pre-Columbian Americas with any certainty because most surviving histories are Eurocentric, generalized, and super biased. We do know that, before the Spaniards planted their colonialist flags in American soil, there were between two and ten million Native Americans living in what is today the continental United States alone. Which is a big range, but pretty effectively demonstrates that there were already a lot of people there. Most natives were organized into tribes, led by chiefs, that united into confederacies. They had no classical-style civilizations like the Inca or Aztec, no metalwork, gunpowder, written language, wheels, horses, or any domesticated animal—except small, often hairless dogs like the Xolo (remember that weirdo? We talked about him a few chapters back too). What they did have was farming, social and political structures, trade networks. They lived off the natural resources available in their area and considered land a common resource assigned for use but not ownership. They were generally spiritual, and most tribes believed not in a single deity but many lesser deities, unlike the monotheistic Europeans.

Because their societal structure was different, it was easy for Europeans like Columbus to see them as both a simple people and a savage, primitive one that need to either be civilized or destroyed.

Some things about Columbus we need to get straight before we go on: First, he didn't think the earth was flat. People knew the earth was round since the Ancient Greeks and Romans. Second, he was definitely not the first European to set foot on American soil. The Vikings had already done that, though they don't get a catchy rhyme. Third, Columbus didn't make one trip to the New

World in 1492 (also, that world wasn't new). He made four total journeys. During his first, which you probably learned about in elementary school, he landed on San Salvador, looking for gold, a quicker route to the Orient to get some of that sweet, sweet spice money, and places to spread Christianity. He brought three ships with him and claimed to come in peace. On his second, he returned with seventeen ships, twelve hundred men, horses, and twenty war dogs, which kind of cancels out the whole peace thing.

War dogs had been previously discovered by European invaders in the Canary Islands to be the most effective way of fighting native populations who possessed no armor, when dogs were used to quell the previously unconquerable Guanches and the Moors of Grenada. According to accounts of the time, the mastiffs used by the Spanish could weigh up to 250 pounds and were three feet high at their shoulder, though there's likely some exaggeration for dramatic effect there. Greyhounds were also used in battle because of their speed. They were trained to chase down men and use slashing attacks to disembowel them.

The Native Americans had never seen huge dogs like those that were brought from Europe. They thought the dogs might be some species of dragon—an impression magnified by the fact that the Spanish dogs arrived armored in chain mail and steel plate like their masters and were thus almost invulnerable to stone weapons. The dogs were denied food before battle so they were super hangry and thus more motivated to attack when they were released onto the battlefield. There are also very easy-to-believe stories that the Spanish soldiers would often set their dogs on the natives just for

fun, or so that they could bet on the outcome. Because they were the wooooooorst.

When Columbus returned to present-day Jamaica, determined to show off the Spanish strength to the Native Americans, it was the war dogs that most effectively terrified them. As he worked his way through Hispaniola, demanding the chiefs surrender to him, he had his dogs at his side, and used them to instill fear in the population. Columbus set the standard for using war dogs against native populations of America. Cortés, de Soto, Pizarro, Vásquez de Coronado, and Balboa also brought dogs with them on their colonizing adventures.

Look, obviously I am not on board with colonization, but if you're going to do it, dear Lord, please don't make dogs complicit in your terrible life choices!

One of the most famous war dogs was named Becerrillo, which means "little bull calf." Becerrillo belonged to Ponce de León, who arrived in modern Florida in 1513, looking for gold, the fountain of youth, and to set up fortifications to protect Spanish galleons sailing out of Mexico from pirates. He was only successful at that last one. He also brought missionaries who came to convert the Native Americans, a conversion that literally no one asked for and so often devolved into aggressive conversion. In general, no one in the Americas really asked for or wanted Ponce de León. And yet there he was, with his guns, horses, and war dogs like Becerrillo.

Becerillo was an enormous mastiff with a bloodthirsty reputation and a body covered in scars from the battles he had survived. He was used to terrorize the natives of Puerto Rico, where Ponce de León had appointed himself governor. He served both on the battlefield and as a soldier and an enforcer of Spanish law in conquered territories. You might say he was Dog the Bounty Hunter—pun intended. As recognition for his service he was treated like a high-ranking soldier—he even received part of the spoils of war. He did not, however, rape and brutalize native women as part of these spoils—that was just the humans. Even at their worst, dogs really are so much better than us.

ACCORDING TO ACCOUNTS OF THE TIME, THE MASTIFFS USED BY THE SPANISH COULD WEIGH UP TO 250 POUNDS AND WERE THREE FEET HIGH AT THEIR SHOULDER.

The most famous story about Becerrillo, however, is the story of his death, and how, in spite of his warrior training, his lovely dog nature won out.

The story goes that Becerrillo's handler, Salazar, sent an old native woman he picked at random off the street to deliver a message for the governor or face certain death. The terrified woman began to walk, but as soon as she was on her way, Salazar ordered Becerrillo to attack her—just for the hell of it, because there was no message, and the Spanish conquerors were JERKS.

Just as he had been trained, Becerrillo chased the woman down. When he caught up to her, she fell on her knees and begged for mercy.

And Becerrillo stopped.

According to multiple accounts, the terror of the Spanish seas, massacrer of the battlefield, stopped, sniffed the woman gently, then turned away without harming her.

We don't know what happened to Becerrillo after that, but his gesture of mercy was likely his last. Based on all previous accounts of Ponce de León's douchebaggery, and the fact that Becerrillo doesn't appear in any records after this incident, when he was told what had occurred, de León likely had Becerrillo killed.

Even when bred for battle and made unwilling accomplices in murder, genocide, and general atrocities against humanity, dogs are gonna dog.

TINKER TAILOR SOLDIER PUG

How One Dog Stopped a Royal Assassination

PUG · NETHERLANDS · 1500s

In the 1500s, the Netherlands were under the control of the Habsburg family, specifically Philip II, the Habsburg king of Spain. And they were getting fed up with being under Spanish rule. The Seventeen Provinces, as the Netherlands of today were known, were wealthy, so they were taxed heavily by their Spanish overlords. They were also subject to Philip's tyrannical devotion to Catholicism and the good Christian theory of conversion by murder. The Spanish Inquisition had come north, and both Protestants and Catholics who weren't Catholic enough were being executed for heresy.

Many members of the nobility were against this policy of Christianity by murder, partly because they were decent people and also partly because they were Calvinists and thus didn't want to get murdered. Among this group was William of Orange, known also as William the Silent. When his religious dissidence and rejection of Spanish rule made him a target of the Inquisition, William managed to escape to the Holy Roman Empire, where he mustered an army to lead against the Spanish for control of the Seventeen Provinces. And thus began the Dutch Revolt and the Eighty Years' War.

William led pirates called the Sea Beggars in raids against the Spanish navy and reclaimed Dutch towns (this strategy of becoming friends with pirates would soon be adopted by Queen Elizabeth I in her own fight against Spain). Inspired by the success of William and his motley crew, the Dutch flocked to join the rebellion. In 1581, the Seventeen Provinces declared independence from Spain, and in 1588 they formed the Republic of the Seven United Netherlands under one government. This made it possible for the Dutch to expand trade, which led to the establishment of the Dutch East India Company, which led to an establishment of the middle class in the Netherlands, which led to the first recorded economic bubble . . .

But I'm getting ahead of myself. History is a chain reaction—it's so cool. Let's talk about the dogs!

Like most European nobles at the time, William had many dogs—some for hunting and other, smaller ones as indoor companions. He often took his dogs to the battle camps with him and kept them in his tent for company. They were not war dogs like the molossuses of the conquistadors; they were meant to provide comfort after battle. One of his favorite canine companions was a pug called Pompey.

One night, while camped at Hermigny, during the Siege of Mons, a Spanish assassin snuck into the Dutch camp and attempted to snuff William in his sleep. While William snored in blissful ignorance, Pompey heard the unknown person approaching their tent and began barking furiously and jumping on his master's face. Whether he was barking because DANGER or barking because POSSIBLE NEW FRIEND, we'll never know, but his commotion woke William, and he was able to escape assassination.

However, only two years later, another assassin caught William unawares, and he was killed in his home in Delft. Pompey was so devastated by the loss of his master, he died three days later. William's mausoleum in the Nieuwe Kerk in Delft depicts Pompey reclining at his master's feet.

WHETHER HE WAS BARKING BECAUSE DANGER OR BARKING BECAUSE POSSIBLE NEW FRIEND, WE'LL NEVER KNOW, BUT HIS COMMOTION WOKE WILLIAM, AND HE WAS ABLE TO ESCAPE ASSASSINATION.

William's ancestors remained devoted to pugs after his death, and the pug became the official dog of the House of Orange. When William the Silent's successor, William III, became joint ruler of England through his marriage to Mary II, their pugs attended the coronation wearing velvet ribbons.

You don't choose the pug life, man. The pug life chooses you.

---

sidebark

The collective noun for a group of pugs is a *grumble*.

Around 1740, Roman Catholics formed a secret group called the Order of the Pug. It was basically an alternate version of the Freemasons, which the Pope had forbidden Catholics from joining. Members were expected to prove their devotion by kissing the Grand Pug under his tail (thank God the Grand Pug was a statue, but still, germs). The members also wore dog collars, scratched at the lodge door for entry, and sometimes barked. The group eventually fizzled out, but you bet I would read a Dan Brown–style novel where Robert Langdon goes hunting for the lost relics of the Order of the Pug.

URIAN THE GREYHOUND

One Dog Chomps the Catholic Church

GREYHOUND · ROME AND ENGLAND · 1520s

Almost everyone knows Henry VIII for one thing: W-I-V-E-S.

Specifically, beheaded wives.

If you know another thing about him, it's probably that this habit of wedding and beheading led to England breaking with Catholicism and the formation of the Anglican Church.

What you probably don't know is that, without one particular dog, that break of church and state may never have happened.

To set the scene: The War of the Roses had just ended. Richard III, having failed to trade his kingdom for a horse, was killed in the Battle of Bosworth in 1485, thus ending the pettiest war of all time, centered around the question of whether the House of York or the House of Lancaster had rightful claim to the English throne.

There was a new house in town—the House of Tudor.

Henry VII took the throne and immediately established a strong dynasty no one could mess with. One of the ways he went about this was by signing a treaty with the region of Aragon, which is in Spain and not the *Lord of the Rings* character, that arranged a marriage between Catherine of Aragon and Henry's son Arthur.

You definitely thought I was going to say his son Henry VIII, didn't you? Hold on. He's coming.

Shortly after his marriage, Arthur died, forever robbing England of having an actual King Arthur on their throne. To preserve their treaty with Aragon, Henry VII began petitioning for Catherine to remarry his other son, also named Henry (there he is). The only problem was that the church had declared it was illegal to marry your brother's widow. But when Henry VII died and the need for a king and a queen became pressing, the rules were bent. Son Henry married Catherine, thereby crowning him King Henry VIII and her Queen Catherine of Aragon.

Henry wanted to be a warrior king. He didn't have time to be doing silly things like worrying about taxes. Real kings fight wars! So he appointed Cardinal Thomas Wolsey to run England while he battled France for Reasons. Wolsey became so powerful he was known as *alter rex*, which means "the other king."

But Wolsey couldn't solve all of Henry's domestic problems. Particularly those in the bedroom. Catherine had five children, only one of which hadn't died, and that one was a dumb, useless, unable-to-inherit-a-kingship girl. Oh, history, you sexist son of a bitch. Henry became convinced that this lack of a male heir was God's way of punishing him for his illegitimate marriage, and that because the marriage had never been legitimate, it didn't need to be divorced—it could be annulled.

This timing also may have also been influenced by the fact that Henry was getting into the bone zone with one of Catherine's maids of honor, Anne Boleyn.

ALL IT TOOK WAS ONE CHOMP FROM URIAN TO SET IN MOTION A SERIES OF EVENTS THAT WOULD CHANGE THE WORLD.

In order to annul his marriage, Henry needed the permission of the Pope. "No problem," said Henry, "the Pope loves me!" Henry sent his royal gopher—who was conveniently also the Pope's official BFF—Wolsey, to Rome to deal with it.

And Wolsey brought along one h*ckin' good boy—his greyhound, Urian.

Greyhounds are the oldest purebred dog still in existence today—they date back to Ancient Egypt, and they appear in both Greek and Roman mythology, as well as the Bible. All of today's sight hounds—meaning hounds that hunt by sight rather than sound—are descended from greyhounds. Until the 1700s in Europe, only the nobility, such as our buddy Wolsey, were allowed to own greyhounds.

For some reason, Urian was not only taken all the way to Rome, he was also invited into Wolsey's audience with the Pope, which makes me feel less like an extra white lady over my insistence that it's fine I take my dog into Anthropologie. The meeting began with a symbolic ceremony in which the Pope extended his bare foot and Wolsey was meant to kiss it.

However, Urian, thinking his master was in danger of being kicked/exposed to terrible Pope foot smell, did a protect. Before Wolsey could kiss the pontific toes, Urian leapt forward in defense and bit the Pope on the foot.

The meeting went downhill from there.

Wolsey was sent back to England with no annulment granted. While Urian's bad behavior might have been the final straw, another large part of the reason the Pope refused to grant the annulment was the Holy Roman Emperor, Charles V. Charles had captured Rome, and just happened to be nephew to our friend Queen Catherine of Aragon, so he had a vested interest in keeping her on the throne of England.

Henry VIII promptly fired Wolsey, appointed a new Archbishop of Canterbury after a series of job interviews that could basically be summed up by one question: Will you proclaim my marriage to Catherine null and void? Once the new archbishop declared him officially a single man in the eyes of God, Henry immediately married Anne, partly because she was a tiny bit pregnant, and if that kid was a boy, it would be really helpful for him to not be born out of wedlock.

The Pope responded by excommunicating Henry.

Henry responded by not giving a fork.

All it took was one chomp from Urian to set in motion a series of events that would

change the world. Henry declared that the Catholic Church couldn't fire him because he quit, and he was going to start his own church—the Church of England. The English Parliament was jazzed about the split with Rome, partly because the church had a lot of land and power that they definitely wanted. The dissolution of the monasteries in 1593 caused a huge chunk of church money and land to be turned over to the government, resulting in the greatest land grab of modern history. The landed gentry became even more powerful. They passed several acts that placed Henry at the head of the church, made it illegal to be Catholic, and decreed it treasonous to disagree. Catherine's only surviving child, Mary, was declared illegitimate and Henry's marriage to Anne and any heirs she might produce the only thing that mattered (foreshadowing).

It's impossible to claim that the break between England and the Catholic Church was triggered by one king wanting a divorce. The seeds of their breakup were planted for almost a century before it actually happened. Thanks to the invention of the printing press, which allowed religious texts to be distributed widely, as well as the writings of men like Martin Luther and Desiderius Erasmus, who had been calling for reformation within the church, England, like all of Europe, was in the middle of huge religious changes.

But without the mighty chomp from Urian, who knows how much longer it might have taken?

---

sidebark

 According to England's Canute Laws, which were passed around 1014, anyone responsible for a greyhound's death could be executed.

 Greyhounds were bred for racing, and can run at speeds of up to forty-five miles per hour.

GAME OF BONES

The Dogs of the English Civil War

HOUNDS · ENGLAND · 1642–1651

I'm going to be honest—the English Civil War is a bitch to explain (no offense to female dogs). I'm going to do my best to tell it to you in dogs.

So it's the early 1600s in England. James I is on the throne, and James had a few issues going into his kingship. First was his absolute, unshakable belief in the divine right of kings, meaning that he was pretty sure he was God. And no one puts God in a corner. So James was not great at listening to anyone. Particularly his parliament—James came from Scotland, which had a parliament as weak as American tea.

The other big problem was that he didn't really care about poor people.

This was obvious in his hunting. Hunting was not something the nobility did to survive—it was a sport. And James believed in the royal prerogative to hunt. James loved hunting, and he loved doing it on the grounds of farmers and common landowners. He would demand his subjects plow their fields in a certain way to best facilitate his hunt rather than the actual farming they needed to survive, then ask that they drop everything and give him and his royal hunting bros whatever they needed, without compensation. These demands ranged

from lodging to everything they needed for a feast and an all-night rager.

James also stole peasants' dogs. In 1616, he gave his royal hound master (#dreamjob) permission to seize any dog and press-gang it into the royal hunting party. Sometimes he would order commoners' dogs killed simply so they wouldn't compete for game with his own hounds. And, cementing his reputation as total trash, James was also an avid fan of the worst sport ever—bearbaiting—and would dognap puppers to fight *Hunger Games*-style against a bear while nobility placed bets on the outcome.

I know, it's atrocious. The 1600s were not a great time to be poor, or a dog. Or a poor dog.

James's son Charles had the same passions for sports that involved killing things as his dad. When he took the throne, he decided that his sixty-eight royal forests were not enough hunting ground, so he seized even more from the common folk and demanded that all dogs that lived there be either mutilated or killed so they could not interfere with the royal hunt.

I know, I'm also ready to lead a revolution at this point. It'll happen.

Charles I also hated being told what to do. Whenever his parliament disagreed

with his life choices, he'd dismiss them, government-shutdown-style. Eventually, the parliament got sick of this and began to fight back, which led to Charles trying to arrest his own parliament, which led to Parliament literally passing declarations about how much Charles sucked. This strife led to a split between people in England who supported the king—aka the Royalists or Cavaliers—and the people who supported Parliament—aka the Roundheads.

THE 1600s WERE NOT A GREAT TIME TO BE POOR, OR A DOG. OR A POOR DOG.

Because of hostilities with the Parliament, Charles fled London and took up a stronghold in Nottingham, officially kicking off the first leg of the English Civil War. One of the key generals on the side of the Royalists was Prince Rupert of the Rhine, and he had a pretty kick-ass sidekick: When he was captured in the Thirty Years' War, he was given a dog for companionship—because just like today, prison is different if you're a rich, white guy. This dog was a white hunting poodle, which sounds fake, but I promise it's real, named Boye. During his captivity, Rupert and Boye became bonded in a way only a man and a dog confined alone to a fairly luxurious tower prison can be. When he was released, Rupert was never seen without Boye. They ate together, they drank together, they slept together, they hunted together. Boye probably mildly creepily watched him go to the bathroom like so many dogs I've known do.

So naturally, when Rupert joined the Royalist cause to quash parliamentary insurrection, they did that together too.

Rupert quickly became one of the most feared and iconic Cavaliers. Boye became as iconic as his master. Because of his distinctive bright white color, he could be seen from the other side of the battlefield, like a looming specter of their impending defeat. With Rupert and Boye at the head of the army, the Royalists clinched several key victories, all of them prefaced by the ghostly appearance across the field of Boye.

The Roundheads were losing the war, and they became convinced it was because of Boye. Parliamentary propaganda began to circulate that Boye had magical powers. Pamphlets were literally being passed around London about the supernatural dog that was the source of all the Royalists' success. He could turn invisible and sneak into their camp to spy. He was the devil in disguise. Rupert was a witch, and Boye his familiar. Some Roundheads even told their soldiers that if they saw Boye, they were to stop whatever they were doing—even if it was fighting their human enemies—and make sure he went down first.

Warning: The dog dies in this one.

At the Battle of Marston Moor, the fate of the Royalists changed. It was their first major military loss—and probably not coincidentally where they also lost their best man, Boye. Though he was tied up in the Royalists' camp, Boye escaped to be near his master once the fighting started, and was killed in battle.

Rupert was devastated. Even he had started to buy into the rumors that Boye made him magically invincible, and when the dog was killed, it affected his whole military strategy. He became more cautious, less decisive. The whole Royalist army suffered a huge blow to their morale. The Roundheads were overjoyed and convinced that because the devil was no longer on the side of the Royalists in the form of Boye, they could be defeated. At the Battle of Naseby, another key loss for the Royalists, the Roundheads rallied their troops with the chant, "Rupert's white witch is dead! They can be defeated!"

After the death of Boye, Rupert never won another victory against the Roundheads. The Royalists lost the war, and Charles I was executed.

But the English Civil War was far from over.

. . . That's another story.

sidebark

Oliver Cromwell, the most famous leader of the Roundheads, later made himself the Lord Protector of the Commonwealth (basically a king by any other name). He died at age fifty-nine, but two years later, when Charles I's son returned to England to reinstate himself and get rid of this Lord Protector BS, Cromwell's body was exhumed just so that he could be executed. In spite of being already dead. Which is pretty h*ckin' extra if you ask me.

The poodle traces its origins to Germany. The name *poodle* comes from the German word *pudel*, or "puddle," which refers to dogs splashing in puddles of water when they would retrieve the waterfowl shot down by hunters. The first poodles were all larger dogs, weighing from forty to seventy pounds.

The weird but iconic hairdo of the poodle actually serves a practical purpose and dates back to the seventeenth century. Their job of retrieving waterfowl often involved jumping into freezing-cold water, but their wet fur weighed them down. Hunters would strategically shear their dogs to lighten the weight, but kept the fur thick where it would protect vital areas and joints from the cold.

THE GRAVITY OF THE SITUATION

In Which Isaac Newton's Dog Almost Ruins Everything

POMERANIAN · ENGLAND · 1642–1727

We all know that the story of the apple falling onto Newton's head and him shouting "Eureka!" and inventing gravity is a myth. But there's a much more interesting backstory to the discovery of one of the universe's basic principles by Sir Isaac, and of course it involves his dog.

Isaac Newton was a key figure in the Scientific Revolution, a period in European history that is considered the emergence of modern scientific fields such as mathematics, physics, astronomy, biology, human anatomy, and chemistry. The Scientific Revolution took place in Europe toward the end of the Renaissance period and continued through the late eighteenth century, where it evolved into the intellectual social movement known as the Enlightenment. While its dates are debated, Nicolaus Copernicus's publication of *De revolutionibus orbium coelestium* (*On the Revolutions of the Heavenly Spheres*), which proposed a heliocentric model of the universe with the sun, rather than the earth, at its center, is often cited as marking the beginning of the Scientific Revolution in 1543.

Initially the focus was on the recovery of the knowledge of the ancients, much

of which had been suppressed during the Middle Ages. In 1632, with the publication of Galileo's *Dialogue Concerning the Two Chief World Systems*, the revolution shifted to new schools of thought. One of the crowning pieces was the publication of Isaac Newton's *Philosophiæ Naturalis Principia Mathematica* in 1687, which included, among other things, our modern understanding of the laws of gravity and the three laws of motion that form the basis of modern physics and mechanics.

But the concepts in *Principia* were very nearly lost to history.

Because of a dog.

Isaac Newton had a cream-colored Pomeranian named Diamond who kept him company while he worked. In several letters, Newton later recounted the following story about his dog: One night, Newton was making final revisions to his treaties by candlelight with Diamond at his feet. Someone knocked on the door, and Newton got up to answer it, and Diamond, as is the great tradition of the dog, went berserk because someone was at the door. Newton left Diamond in the study, where she proceeded to run circles.

On one of these laps around the room, Diamond collided with the leg of Newton's writing table, which tipped the candle over. Directly onto the manuscript. So Newton returned to the study to find twenty years of research literally up in flames.

The manuscript that Newton was working on was completely destroyed.

But rather than hanging a sign around Diamond's neck that said "i destroyed my person's monumental scientific research that will shape the twentieth century because i am a smol dog and am thus made of chaotic energy" and posting it to ye olde dog-shaming Instagram, he is said to have picked up his dog and said, "Oh, Diamond, Diamond, little do you know the mischief you have done me!"

The fire, however, was harder to shake off than that flippant statement would suggest.

The loss sent Newton into a depression that took him months to recover from. He stayed in bed for several weeks after the incident, though he wrote that Diamond stayed in the bed with him, so no hard feelings. It would be a year before he could reconstruct the theory of gravity, but, happy ending—Newton published his theories and the rest is history.

Later in life, Newton became more and more prone to these periods of depression and mania and suffered a nervous breakdown in 1693. But a 1979 examination of Newton's hair showed amounts of mercury were in his system, which was probably affecting his mental stability. The mercury was a result of all his alchemy experiments and his attempt to create a philosopher's stone.

But that's another book. About Harry Potter.

sidebark

In Newton's time, Pomeranians were not the ten-pound teacups we know today. They were still evolving. Poms are descended from arctic sled dogs and are part of a group called spitz breeds, which is a type of dog that has several wolflike physical characteristics, including long, thick, and often white fur, and pointed ears and muzzles. Other breeds that fall into this category include the Alaskan malamute, the Akita, the Samoyed, and the Norwegian elkhound. Pomeranians were bred as working dogs, and originally weighed an average of thirty pounds. In the nineteenth century, when dogs became much more popular as companion animals for the rich, thanks in part to Queen Victoria's love for them, they were bred smaller for convenience. However, the gene for enormousness is still present in the breed: Sometimes breeders will get a "throwback" Pom that ends up giant.

Pomeranians are probably from Iceland, but are named for a small region in northeast Germany—Pomerania, which is where the breed began to take on its modern characteristics.

Aside from Queen Victoria (who at one point had thirty-five in the royal kennels), history is full of Pom fans. Mozart dedicated one of his arias to his pet Pomeranian, Pimperl. Chopin was inspired to write "Waltz of the Little Dogs" by his friend's Pomeranian chasing his tail. When Michelangelo was painting the Sistine Chapel, his Pom was sitting below watching the action.

THE DOG SHOGUN

Protecting the Strays of Japan

JAPAN · 1600s

Were I queen of the world, 99 percent of my decrees would benefit dogs.

There's a reason I'm not queen, which is that this is a terrible way to run the world.

But I would not be the first ruler in history to focus all my efforts on my four-legged citizens.

Meet Tokugawa Tsunayoshi, the dog shogun of Japan.

First, what is a shogun? The shoguns were the hereditary officials who governed Japan, with the emperor serving over all of them. They were the military dictators of feudal Japan from 1185 to 1868, and through the vast military resources at their disposal, they were absolute rulers.

Tsunayoshi was part of the Tokugawa dynasty, which seized power and established a government at Edo (now known as Tokyo) in 1600. Because he was born in 1646, the year of the dog, Tsunayoshi grew up certain he was a dog in a previous life. The Japanese calendar, much like the Chinese, has a different animal to represent each year in cycles of twelve. People born the year of the dog are known for being champions of moral causes and particularly sensitive to injustice. In 1681, Tsunayoshi became the fifth Tokugawa shogun of Japan, and soon the most divisive as well.

At the time, Japan was obsessed with class. The samurai nobles were kept strictly separate from the agricultural class. And though we now associate samurai with warriors, high positions like scholars, aristocrats, and government officials came from the samurai class too. Samurai was less a type of soldier and more the name for the upper tier of Japanese society who often used military force on their subjects in order to stay on top. They were also obsessed with tradition, because it justified them living large and not caring about normal people.

Tsunayoshi was concerned that the brutal tactics of the samurai had made his people accustomed to being beaten into submission, and that Japan was suffering from a general lack of kindness and tolerance. His studies of Neo-Confucianism, Buddhism, and Taoism, all of which put an emphasis on compassion and charity, led him to pass a series of edicts that can basically be summed up as "just be a decent human." Known by an amazing literal name, the Edicts on Compassion for Living Things, they were released daily to the public of Edo. These included rules like "protect abandoned children" and "give beggars food" and "maybe don't abandon your family members when they get old."

A disproportionate number of these edicts were concerned with animal welfare. Tsunayoshi passed laws that punished animal cruelty first with banishment, then death. At the time, Edo was overrun with dogs. While samurai bred pedigree dogs they used for hunting and companionship, the number of dogs most samurai kept was out of control. Some estates would have hundreds of dogs, which would inevitably lead to unplanned pregnancy, which would then result in the extra dogs either being killed or turned out into the streets, where they became aggressive in order to survive.

Edo was a city of strays.

Since the samurai were living in walled residences, they weren't so concerned about what was happening in the actual city, but the dogs became a health hazard for the common people, particularly when packs started attacking humans. Tsunayoshi tried to curb this problem by passing a law that no dogs were to be abandoned in the streets. He called for dogs to be treated according to "the fundamental principles of humanity"; i.e., not killed for being homeless.

Which sounds reasonable and great. But.

With nothing to keep the dog population in check, Edo became even more overrun with stray dogs. And Tsunayoshi just kept doubling down with his laws protecting them. It got to a point where the shogun's laws became so strict that a dog owner suspected of negligence could be punished. It became a crime to chastise a dog. People were jailed simply for ignoring a stray dog in need. The citizens of Edo were worried

they couldn't defend themselves from stray pack attacks without facing punishment, and began to fear dogs in the same way they feared the brutal, high-ranking samurai officials. Eventually, Tsunayoshi ordered that all dogs had to be addressed as O-inu-sama, which means "most honorable and revered dog." It was a form of address previously reserved only for deities.

The laws had been designed to protect the defenseless doggos of Edo, but instead it had essentially given dogs control of the city.

TSUNAYOSHI ORDERED THAT ALL DOGS HAD TO BE ADDRESSED AS O-INU-SAMA, WHICH MEANS "MOST HONORABLE AND REVERED DOG." IT WAS A FORM OF ADDRESS PREVIOUSLY RESERVED ONLY FOR DEITIES.

So Tsunayoshi came up with a new plan—he had public kennels built for the city's stray dogs, where they would be fed better than most peasants and using taxpayers money. Fifty thousand pups were sent to their new luxury condos, with more added every day. The citizens of Edo were funding the extravagant lifestyles of somewhere between fifty thousand and one hundred thousand stray dogs. Many were forced to abandon their homes to make space for the 230-acre kennels. The samurai were mad because they had more land to tax, so they were paying more, and the agricultural class was mad because they already didn't have a ton of money, so why did they also have to pay for dogs that weren't theirs?

When Tsunayoshi's successor, his nephew Ienobu, took over the shogunship, he immediately abolished the Edicts on Compassion for Living Things relating to animal welfare. No matter how well-meaning Tsunayoshi had been in passing them, Ienobu recognized that the enforcement of the laws had gotten out of hand. The kennels were also destroyed, but no record clearly states the fate of the dogs there.

In spite of how off course his policies went, Tsunayoshi's heart was in the right place, and his spirit lives on in modern Tokyo at Ichigaya Kamegaoka Hachimangu Shrine, where dogs and other pets can receive a Shichi-Go-San ceremony, which traditionally marks ages of transition in the lives of human children. The shrine also offers pet-friendly *hatsumōde* (Japanese New Year) events and has pet-oriented *omamori* (Japanese lucky charms).

I WANT BRANDY!

Barry and the Rescue Dogs of St. Bernard Pass

ST. BERNARD · SWITZERLAND · 1660s

I begin this entry with a disclaimer: I am very fond of this story, due to the fact that a dog of the breed we are about to discuss is currently snoring under my chair as I write these words. But I promise I will be as impartial and objective as possible in my recounting of its history. I am, after all, a professional.

Okay, now the origin story of the greatest dog breed of all time: the St. Bernard.

Great St. Bernard Pass is a forty-nine-mile route between Switzerland and Italy that's only snow-free for a few months out of every year. In order to help struggling trekkers, an Augustine monk named St. Bernard de Menthon founded a hospice and monastery there around the year 1050—hence the name of the pass. The hospice became a place for travelers and pilgrims to rest, warm up, and refresh for the remainder of the journey ahead.

St. Bernards were introduced to the monastery as watchdogs at some point between 1660 and 1670, but were soon put to work on other tasks as well. At the time, these dogs were called Alpenmastiffs or cowherds' dogs. Servants were assigned to accompany travelers between the hospice and Bourg-Saint-Pierre, a nearby city, and the dogs often went with them. Their broad chests and enormous paws helped to clear paths for travelers.

Their sense of smell also gave them the ability to locate people who had been buried in the snow. They were trained to dig out these trapped travelers, then lick and lie on them to restore their body heat. It wasn't long before dogs were sent out in packs to find injured travelers without human assistance. When the pack located the travelers, one dog would run back to the hospice and lead the monks to the rescue site. If a dog was alone, he would lie on the victim and bark until monks arrived.

When not working, the dogs also provided much-needed companionship to travelers at the hospice, and to the monks, because it can get pretty lonely in a remote monastery located along a dangerous Alpine pass that is almost always completely frozen.

In 1800, Barry der Menschenretter (which means "Barry the People Rescuer" because sometimes we are just not very creative) became one of the dogs in residence. He would have stood slightly smaller than the modern St. Bernard—the original rescue dogs would weigh around one hundred pounds, whereas, due to crossbreeding with mastiffs and Newfoundlands, the modern St. Bernard typically weighs in at between 130 and 200 pounds. Barry would have also born a closer resemblance to a modern Labrador, with short, reddish-and-white fur. So, ironically, history's most famous St. Bernard would have looked nothing like today's St. Bernards.

During Barry's career, he was credited with saving the lives of more than forty people, though that number is almost impossible to verify. Barry's most famous rescue was a young boy who he found lost in a cavern of ice. After licking him awake, Barry carried the boy to the hospice on his back. And while I'd rather not get lost in an ice cave, being licked awake and then carried by a giant dog is my ideal way to spend a snow day.

According to the plaque on his monument, Barry died making his forty-first rescue in the pass. Not true. After twelve years of service at the monastery, Barry retired to Bern, Switzerland, where he lived out the rest of his life doing the very important work of the St. Bernard: holding down the floor. Barry's taxidermied body is on display at the Natural History Museum in Bern.

The monks in St. Bernard Pass still breed dogs, though they don't do as much rescuing these days. To honor their famous kin, one puppy from every litter born there is named Barry.

sidebark

 The iconic brandy barrel worn around the neck of St. Bernards wasn't ever used in actual mountain rescue. It was an invention of an artist named Edwin Landseer in the 1820s, in a painting called *Alpine Mastiffs Reanimating a Distressed Traveler*. Landseer claimed the barrel he painted around one of the dog's necks contained brandy to revive the traveler. The truth is that brandy isn't something you'd want if you were buried in an avalanche. Alcohol causes blood vessels to dilate, resulting in blood rushing to your skin and your body temperature decreasing rapidly.

 In 1800, the monks and their St. Bernards assisted Napoleon's troops in crossing the pass. Not a single soldier lost his life.

In 1830, the monks started breeding their St. Bernards with Newfoundlands in an attempt to create coats with longer hair that were more suited for the environment. This plan backfired: Their coats were longer, but ice clung to the hair and weighed the dogs down, making rescues more difficult. However, these unsuccessful Newf-Saint hybrids, which were given to people living in the nearby valleys, paved the way for the modern look of today's Saints.

The collective noun for a group of St. Bernards is a floof (I PROMISE I DIDN'T JUST MAKE THAT UP THOUGH THAT DEFINITELY SOUNDS LIKE SOMETHING I WOULD DO).

"IF YOU WANT A FRIEND IN WASHINGTON, GET A DOG"

First Pups in the White House

UNITED STATES

Almost every POTUS has had a pet in the White House. Dogs in particular have been kept by presidents and adored by the public—and led to more than a few memorable presidential moments.

Here are some facts to satisfy your curipawsity about the First Dogs of the United States:

George Washington

🐾 Washington had dozens of dogs over his lifetime, all of which had amazing names, including Sweetlips (which I'm convinced was also Washington's drag name), Scentwell, True Love, and Madame Moose, as well as Taster, Tipler, Tipsy, and Drunkard. There's a chance these dogs had a drinking problem.

🐾 During the Revolutionary War, Washington found a dog belonging to British general William Howe on the battlefield of Germantown, and went to great lengths to make sure he was returned. Despite being on different sides of the conflict, they had their dogs in common.

🐾 Washington was a passionate breeder of hunting hounds, and, in trying to breed a superior dog with speed, sense, and brains, he created the American foxhound.

Theodore Roosevelt

🐾 The Roosevelts win the award for "White House Most Resembling a Zoo." Their pets included a host of dogs, as well as guinea pigs, chickens, ponies, lizards, macaws, a snake named Emily Spinach, a black bear, piebald rats, badgers, pigs, rabbits, a hyena, owls, and a one-legged rooster.

🐾 Roosevelt's bull terrier Pete almost caused an international scandal when he ripped the pants off the French ambassador, Jules Jusserand. Not long after, Pete was exiled from the White House to the family home on Long Island.

Warren G. Harding

🐾 Laddie Boy, Harding's Airedale, was the first presidential dog to receive wide coverage in the press. He even had his own hand-carved chair, which he'd sit in during cabinet meetings. Harding would also pen letters to the press, writing as Laddie Boy sharing his canine opinions on various political topics, and the press would stage mock interviews with the dog.

❀ After Harding's death, pennies were donated from newsboys across the nation (Harding's first job was as a newsboy) to be melted down and formed into a statue of Laddie Boy. Made of more than nineteen thousand pennies, that statue is now in the Smithsonian.

Franklin D. Roosevelt

❀ FDR's most famous dog was the Scottish terrier Murray the Outlaw of Falahill, or Fala for short. The dog was named after one of FDR's Scottish ancestors.

FALA IS THE ONLY PRESIDENTIAL PET TO BE INCLUDED IN A NATIONAL MONUMENT— HE'S IMMORTALIZED ALONG WITH FDR ON THE NATIONAL MALL.

❀ During the war, Fala gave one dollar a day to the war effort, earning him the rank of honorary private in the army.

❀ When Roosevelt campaigned for reelection in 1944, Republicans accused him of accidentally leaving the First Dog in the Aleutian Islands, then sending a naval destroyer to pick him up, wasting thousands of taxpayer dollars. The story was false— obvious to anyone who has ever owned a dog, because, OMG, how do you leave your dog somewhere?! The president responded in a campaign address that went down in history as the Fala Speech. He said that he didn't resent Republican attacks, "But Fala does resent them . . . his Scotch soul was furious. He has not been the same dog since." The Fala Speech helped revive Roosevelt's campaign, and he went on to win a fourth term in the White House.

❀ Fala is the only presidential pet to be included in a national monument— he's immortalized along with FDR on the National Mall.

John F. Kennedy

❀ During the Cold War, the Kennedys were given a dog by Soviet Union premier Nikita Khrushchev. Her name was Pushinka (Russian for "fluffy"), and she was the offspring of Soviet space dog Strelka. It was a bit of a shady reminder that the Soviet Union was ahead in the space race, having launched *Sputnik* in 1957. There was also some suspicion that Pushinka was a Russian spy, and she had to be thoroughly patted down by the Secret Service for electronic bugs before she was allowed into the White House. She blended well into the Kennedy family and hit it off so well with Caroline Kennedy's Welsh terrier Charlie that in 1963 she gave birth to a litter of puppies that the president called "pupniks," which is perhaps the greatest portmanteau of the modern world.

❀ JFK was also the only president to formally request that his dogs greet him when he arrived home via helicopter.

❀ Charlie was a huge comfort to Kennedy during the Cuban Missile Crisis. In October 1962, the world was teetering on the

brink of nuclear war after the Soviet Union deployed several ballistic missiles on Cuba. Kennedy was trying to figure out how to get the missiles out of Cuba without starting a nuclear war, while the whole country was crouched under their desks in the fallout position, anticipating nuclear winter. In the Situation Room at the White House, Charlie sat on the president's lap as Kennedy made critical decisions about what actions to take. Those in the room said the dog's presence had a visibly calming effect on Kennedy, who successfully navigated the crisis, all while giving Charlie good scritches.

Lyndon B. Johnson

❧ Yuki, President Johnson's mixed-breed dog, was known for her singing and her intense bond with President Johnson. They'd swim together, sleep together, and they even danced together at his daughter Lynda's wedding. The First Lady had to convince President Johnson that the dog did not need to be in the wedding pictures—"But why?" asks this author.

❧ Five other dogs served their time in the White House while President Johnson was in office, two of which caused a scandal. When Johnson was photographed lifting up one of his beagles, Him, by his ears on the White House lawn, animal lovers across the country were outraged. Johnson shrugged off the criticism and said that that's how beagles were meant to be held. Seems fake, but okay.

Gerald Ford

❧ President Ford's golden retriever, Liberty, may be the only presidential dog to send the Secret Service into full-blown

crisis mode. One evening, the president decided to handle dog duty himself, which involved a late-night trip to the South Lawn for what my puppy and I refer to as "tinkle time" (we are classy bitches). Except he forgot to tell his security, and the two of them ended up locked out of the White House.

Richard Nixon

❧ Shortly after presidential candidate Dwight D. Eisenhower chose Nixon as his running mate, the New York Post ran an article claiming that campaign donors were buying influence with Nixon by keeping a secret fund stocked with cash for his personal expenses, and he should be taken off the ticket as a result. Nixon had to submit to a thorough audit of his spending and took to national television to defend himself against the accusation. The most famous part of the speech, however, was when Nixon admitted that his cocker spaniel, Checkers, had been a gift from a supporter, but he wasn't about to give up the pup—his daughters loved Checkers too much. That moment of humanity—and the invocation of man's best friend—may have swayed public opinion on Nixon, and he and Eisenhower won the election.

❧ After Checkers died, Nixon had three dogs at the White House—an Irish setter, a Yorkie, and a poodle. He also kept a drawer full of dog biscuits in his Oval Office desk.

The Bushes

❧ The dogs of both George H. W. (number forty-one) and George W. (number forty-three) were celebrities during their time in the White House. Number forty-one's most famous pup was an English springer spaniel named Millie, whose debut memoir, *Millie's Book: As Dictated to Barbara Bush*, outsold Barbara's autobiography. The book was a *New York Times* bestseller, and raised more than one million dollars for literacy programs.

❀ Number forty-three wasn't the only second-generation Bush to make it to the White House. His English springer spaniel, Spot, was the daughter of Millie. This made Spot the only second-generation pet in White House history.

NUMBER FORTY-ONE'S MOST FAMOUS PUP WAS AN ENGLISH SPRINGER SPANIEL NAMED MILLIE, WHOSE DEBUT MEMOIR, *MILLIE'S BOOK: AS DICTATED TO BARBARA BUSH,* OUTSOLD BARBARA'S AUTOBIOGRAPHY.

Barack Obama

❀ During his 2008 campaign, America's dad, President Obama, promised his daughters, Sasha and Malia, that they would get a dog if he won. They chose a Portuguese water dog because the breed is hypoallergenic and Malia is allergic. After Obama's reelection, Bo was joined by another Portie named Sunny.

❀ Sunny and Bo met a lot of famous people in their tenure as White House dogs, but none went viral quite like their meeting with Pope Francis, who is named for the patron saint of animals.

❀ Portuguese water dogs were historically tasked with seafaring, thanks to their webbed toes. They herded fish into nets, retrieved lost or broken nets, and worked as canine couriers from ship to shore. But the breed nearly went extinct after fishers began upgrading to more advanced equipment at the end of the nineteenth century. A Portuguese businessman named Vasco Bensaude helped revive the breed in the 1930s. After the Obamas adopted Bo, the demand for Porties in the United States hit an all-time high.

FORTUNE THE PUG

Napoleon Bonaparte Has a Bone to Pick with Dogs

PUG · FRANCE · 1769–1821

In spite of the fact that his name has so much potential for canine puns (see: the title of this chapter), Napoleon Bonaparte hated dogs. But that didn't stop dogs from playing a surprisingly large role in the life of history's smallest general. (Though that's just a myth—at five seven, Napoleon was average height for a Frenchman in the 1700s.)

Before we get to the dogs, let me give you a little context for the world that allowed Napoleon to appoint himself Supreme Leader of Any Part of Europe He Could Get His Hands On.

In the late 1700s, the population of France was divided into three groups: nobles, clergy, and everyone else. The everyone else was getting sick of the 1 percent, who forced the general population to pay taxes while both the nobility and clergy were exempt. When King Louis XVI gathered representatives from each group to discuss this, all three groups were given equal vote, in spite of the everyone else vastly outnumbering the clergy and nobles. And of course the clergy and nobles voted to continue not taxing themselves. The common folk were furious—there was also a food shortage, so they were probably hangry—and in response, formed the National Assembly, which they declared

to be the new government of France. The National Assembly then passed the Declaration of the Rights of Man and Citizen, which basically said that we all get life, liberty, and property, and that these rights were intrinsic.

And bang! We have a French Revolution.

It wasn't long before rifts began to form within the National Assembly. When Louis was caught trying to escape France, the question of what to do about the king split the rebels. The more moderate thought the constitutional monarchy should stick around. The radical Jacobins, such as the infamous Robespierre, wanted the king out of the picture entirely. Eventually, the Jacobins took over control of the government and drafted a new constitution. Which seems like a good thing, but the Jacobins were starting to get paranoid, both outside threats—Austria had come out in support of Louis (because his queen, Marie Antoinette, was Austrian)—and internal threats, which is why they started chopping off noble heads, just to be safe. Then chopping off the heads of anyone, just to be safe. The revolution climaxed with the Reign of Terror, when fifteen thousand people were executed by orders of the newly formed Committee of Public Safety, the most ironically named governing board in history.

One of those executed nobles was Alexandre de Beauharnais, the first husband of the woman who would become Empress Joséphine Bonaparte. Joséphine was also imprisoned and scheduled for execution. While she was in prison, no one was allowed to communicate with her. But her pet pug, Fortune, would come visit her every day. The guards didn't pay much attention to the snarfling little dog, so Joséphine was able to smuggle messages under his collar to people on the outside who were then able to intervene in her execution.

By this time, the French government was a wreck. One of the only things that was working was the war effort against Austria, thanks in large part to the tactics of Napoleon Bonaparte. When Joséphine and Napoleon met in 1795, he was already a noted general with a reputation for keeping down revolts, and she was a widow with a reputation for sleeping around because the things men and women are remembered for in history are super fun and sexist. He was six years younger than her, and his family disapproved, but four months after they met, they were married.

You know who else disapproved? Fortune the pug.

Fortune slept in bed with Joséphine every night, and was prepared to do the same on her wedding night. Except there was a *man* in the bed. A man in flagrante delicto with his human. So Fortune did the only logical thing: He leapt into the fray and bit Napoleon, leaving scars the general would carry for the rest of his life. Napoleon was furious and told Joséphine that the dog would no longer be sharing their bed. Joséphine replied that if Fortune couldn't sleep with Napoleon, neither would she.

Fortune got the bed.

Two days after the wedding, Napoleon left Paris to lead the French army into Italy in their continuing campaign to quash outside threats to the fragile new government. His campaign saw successes (in Italy) and failures (in Egypt). While he was gone, he wrote love letters to Joséphine back in Paris, where she was living the high life. When Napoleon because suspicious his wife was cheating on him (she was), he sent for her to join him in Italy, hoping absence would make the heart grow less interested in hot side pieces.

No problem—Joséphine brought her lover with her. And her other great love, Fortune. Obvs.

Tragically, Fortune was killed in a scuffle with another dog, leaving Joséphine devastated. But her boyfriend bought her a new pug, which she also named Fortune, thereby totally confirming Napoleon's suspicions of an affair, because you don't buy a girl a pug unless you're serious about her.

Napoleon really hated dogs.

By the time Napoleon and Joséphine returned to France, Robespierre had been executed, the Reign of Terror ended, and a new government called the Directory was in power. However, they were weak enough that Napoleon and his allies were able to overthrow them and install him as first consul of France.

Napoleon made some great changes. He promoted based on merit, not birth. He reformed army medicine, communication, and supply chains. He also declared that no dogs were allowed to be named Napoleon, but damn, wouldn't that be a great name for a giant Newfoundland? Just to really piss Napoleon off.

Wait, we haven't gotten to the Newfoundlands yet. Hold on, this joke is funny. You'll see.

In 1804, Napoleon was declared emperor. I know, I know, didn't we just fight a revolution to get rid of a monarchy? And yet here we are.

With his coronation, the Napoleonic Wars officially kicked off, in which France tried to systematically wipe out every other governing body in Europe.

And it kind of worked.

Napoleon was a brilliant general and had great luck with conquering European soil. Less so on the water—his army's most iconic defeat was against the British navy at the Battle of Trafalgar. To make matters even more humiliating, the boarding party that took the main French warship was led by a Newfoundland dog. Reports say that when he heard about this, Napoleon cried, "Dogs! Must I be defeated by them on the battlefield as well as in the bedroom?"

Napoleon really hated dogs.

By 1812, most of Europe was controlled by France, and Russia was getting nervous about that. They started trading with Britain again, which they had been expressly told by France not to do because France hated Britain, which was enough to incite France to invade Russia. But, as everyone except Napoleon knows, never get involved in a land war in Asia. The French army was mostly frozen and starving before they could even put up a fight. Napoleon's failure in Russia led to the major European powers forming a coalition against France—their sixth try to stand up to them, and this time it worked. Napoleon abdicated and was exiled to the island of Elba, as in Idris. France became a constitutional monarchy once more.

Napoleon eventually escaped Elba with the intention of initiating a power grab in France again. Ironically, he never would have made it to France if a Newfoundland dog hadn't intervened. When leaving Elba, Napoleon was knocked from the boat into the ocean. He was wearing a heavy uniform and was also not a great swimmer, which is a recipe for drowning. But the ship's Newfoundland dog leapt in after him and did a rescue. He dragged Napoleon to safety, and Napoleon lived to seize the French throne yet again . . . and then lose it at the Battle of Waterloo. A battle he may not have lived to lose if that Newfoundland hadn't dragged him from the sea.

Napoleon mostly hated dogs.

sidebark

Napoleon sold the Louisiana Purchase to America to fund the Napoleonic Wars, particularly an attempted invasion of England. But America borrowed money from British banks to make that purchase. Meaning Britain was basically paying for France to invade them. Which I just find hilarious.

The "canine curse" upon the Bonapartes lasted until the final descendant of Napoleon, Jerome Napoleon Bonaparte, died in 1945 as a result of injuries he sustained when he tripped over his dog while walking it in Central Park. The dog was a pug. *ghost of Fortune snarfle-cackles*

WOOFERS GO WEST!

Lewis, Clark, and Their Newfoundland, Seaman,
Lead the Corps of Discovery

NEWFOUNDLAND · AMERICA · 1804–1806

By the mid-eighteenth century, France controlled more of the present-day United States than any other European power.

That quickly changed when, during the French and Indian War, France ceded French Louisiana west of the Mississippi River to Spain and in 1763 transferred almost all of its remaining North American holdings to Great Britain. But in 1801, Spain signed a secret treaty with France to return the Louisiana Territory in exchange for Tuscany so that Napoleon could sell it to the United States to get some fast cash to fund his conquering of Europe.

And boom. Louisiana—purchased. *cash register sound effect*

The Louisiana Purchase expanded the United States by 828,000 square miles, basically doubling the size of the bb nation. Remember—America is only twenty-seven years old at this point, an age at which most of us are experiencing the emotional equivalent of trying to get one ice cube from the cup into your mouth but then they all fall onto your face. Perhaps we can consider the Louisiana Purchase a result of its mid-quarter-life crisis.

And, as with most impulse buys, America didn't totally know what it was getting into.

The US government knew that what they had just purchased, the Louisiana Territory, stretched from the Mississippi River in the east to the Rocky Mountains in the west and from the Gulf of Mexico in the south to the Canadian border in the north. But beyond that, their knowledge of their new digs was one big shrug emoji. So President Jefferson sent what became known as the Corps of Discovery to, well, discover. The expedition's primary goal was to find a waterway to the Pacific Ocean—the infamous Northwest Passage that everyone was so sure existed (spoiler alert: It doesn't). The expedition was also expected to map the geography and natural life of the region, as well as establish relationships with the Native Americans.

President Jefferson appointed Meriwether Lewis, a militia leader, politician, explorer, and presidential aide, to lead the expedition. At the time, Lewis was twenty-nine years old—the same age of the oldest contestants on this past season of *The Bachelor*, which, sidebar, can we get a *Bachelor* spin-off in which the contestants have to trek their way across the country while falling in love? To prepare for his journey, Lewis studied medicine, botany, astronomy, and zoology. He also added two important members to his team: his cocaptain, William Clark, and his dog, Seaman.

Seaman was a Newfoundland, purchased by Lewis for twenty dollars in Pittsburgh while he was waiting for the completion of the boats that would be taken on the journey. Newfoundlands are named for the Canadian region in which they were a staple on every fishing boat. Known for being strong swimmers, Newfoundlands were used for pulling in nets and retrieving objects and people that fell into the sea (like Napoleon!). Their enormous lung capacity and webbed feet make it possible for them to swim long distances, even against strong currents, and their oily outer coat combined with their fleecy undercoat repels cold water and keeps them warm. Since their company would be traveling on water whenever possible, Lewis wanted a dog that could handle all terrains.

The company set out in May 1804 from St. Louis, Missouri.

Seaman appears infrequently in Lewis's journals, as Lewis was occupied with things like documenting flowers and buffalo and, you know, colonialism, but the Corps's accounts are littered with mentions of Seaman and his antics. One of the first comes before they left Pittsburgh on August 30, 1803. Lewis writes as they traveled down the Ohio River, "[T]he squirrell appears in great abundance on either side of the river. I made my dog take as many each day as I had occasion for, they wer fat and I thought them when fryed a pleasent food."

This was one of many instances in which Seaman's skills as a hunter proved helpful to the Corps. Food was often scarce, particularly in the winter, and they were well outside the delivery range of DoorDash. Though the Corps were forced to eat their horses to survive, they didn't eat Seaman.

However, one of these dinner expeditions almost cost our hero his life. When going to retrieve a beaver that had been shot and wounded by a member of their crew, the beaver bit Seaman in the leg, severing an artery. Don't worry—the dog doesn't die in this one. Both Lewis and Clark took extraordinary measures to save Seaman.

"THE GREATEST TRAVELLER OF MY SPECIES. MY NAME IS SEAMAN, THE DOG OF CAPTAIN MERIWETHER LEWIS, WHOM I ACCOMPANIED TO THE PACIFIC OCEAN THROUGH THE INTERIOR OF THE CONTINENT OF NORTH AMERICA."

Ten days later, Seaman repaid his life debt by saving the entire camp when he redirected the path of a charging buffalo, keeping it from trampling the sleeping company.

On November 15, 1805, Lewis and Clark finally reached the Pacific Ocean. They took some selfies, probably high-fived, then turned around and headed back to tell President Jefferson to stop trying to make the Northwest Passage happen. On their journey, they had discovered hundreds of new species of plants and animals, established mostly positive relationships with the Native Americans in the territory—positive relationships that every other American that came after them would work hard to undo—and created around 140 maps. The journey took two years, four months, and ten days.

And what happened to Seaman? Historians aren't sure. His last appearance in Lewis's journals is on July 15, 1806, but we're pretty sure he survived the trip, because no one ever wrote about him dying. Our best clue comes from Lewis and Clark scholar Jim Holmberg, who discovered a book written in 1814 that listed an inscription on a dog collar in a museum in Virginia reading: "The greatest traveller of my species. My name is SEAMAN, the dog of captain Meriwether Lewis, whom I accompanied to the Pacific ocean through the interior of the continent of North America."

Ah, Seaman. You got the best walkie of all time.

sidebark

Their first winter in what is today North Dakota with the Mandan Indians, Lewis and Clark hired the worst translator in the history of translators—Toussaint Charbonneau, a French-Canadian fur trapper whose name sounds like a pastry. Charbonneau was an all-around dipshit. He refused to pull his weight on the Corps, needed constant rescuing, and didn't really speak the Native American languages he was hired to translate. He had also entered into what several academic papers I read termed a "nonconsensual marriage" but what I like to call "kidnapping and rape" of a Native American woman, who turned out to be the savior of the whole forking expedition. Her name was Sacagawea. One of the more amazing moments of the journey was when the Corps appealed to the Shoshone people for horses to help them cross the Rocky Mountains. The chief was reluctant, until he discovered that Sacagawea was his sister. She had been kidnapped and sold to Charbonneau when she was thirteen years old. This reunion changed the chief's mind, and the Corps was able to get the horses they needed to cross to the Pacific coast.

Lewis and Clark sent President Jefferson a specimen of a rare and exotic animal they found on their journey, which had never been seen before in the east—the elusive and extraordinary prairie dog. No relation to actual dogs.

EPITAPH TO A DOG

MAD, BAD, AND DANGEROUS TO PET

Lord Byron's Dog Boatswain, and Also, What Was the Romantic Movement?

NEWFOUNDLAND · EUROPE · 1788–1824

Many would have volunteered to be the great love of Lord Byron's life: Lady Caroline Lamb; Claire Clairmont; Anne Isabella Milbanke; his half sister, Augusta Leigh; Percy Shelley; most of the population of nineteenth-century London . . .

But none of them could compare to the truest of Byron's true loves: his dog Boatswain.

Boatswain was one of the many pets Lord Byron kept—he enjoyed leaning hard into his eccentric-rock-star image. Over the course of his life, Byron had everything from a tamed bear he kept in his dorm at Trinity College (as a protest against the school's no-dogs rule) to a wolf that roamed the grounds of his ancestral home, Newstead Abbey (which once tore the seat of Byron's breeches off like something out of *Looney Tunes*). In 1821, Percy Shelley cataloged Byron's menagerie at "ten horses, eight enormous dogs, three monkeys, five cats, an eagle, a crow, and a falcon . . . I have just met on the grand staircase five Peacocks, two guinea hens, and an Egyptian crane." All of these animals were allowed to roam his house freely.

He truly was the Romantic Keith Richards.

That's capital-*R* Romantic, by the way. Let's talk about what that means.

Byron was a poet/professional famous person at the height of the Romantic movement. Romanticism emerged in the mid-eighteenth century in Western Europe and quickly spread across the world. While factories were springing up, consumerism was on the rise, and the Enlightenment was favoring reason above all else, a group of primarily artists and thinkers said, "No, we want to feel things!"

The Romantics were all about their *f e e l i n g s*. And since it was eighteenth-century Europe, it was primarily rich white men having these feelings. They had *f e e l i n g s* on a variety of subjects: Wordsworth glorified nature and the natural world in reaction to industrialization. Rousseau exalted childhood as a time of purity and innocence, where previously children had been considered mini adults. And though the word *romantic* in this context didn't carry our modern connotations of the word, the Romantics did believe in following your heart rather than marrying for money, class, or lineage (a lot of them also used this as justification for the practice of free love, or, in a word, cheating).

They pushed the limits of reason. They had sympathy for madness. Just say no to progress and rationality!

This movement made possible the rise of George Gordon Byron Kardashian. Poet, philosopher, philanderer, and a professional celebrity long before Paris Hilton, though his whole life was essentially one big sex tape.

BYRON'S CHILDHOOD FRIEND ELIZABETH PIGOT ILLUSTRATED CARTOONS FEATURING BYRON AND BOATSWAIN'S EXPLOITS AND PUBLISHED THEM IN A CHILDREN'S BOOK CALLED *THE WONDERFUL HISTORY OF LORD BYRON AND HIS DOG.*

Byron was known as much for his Romantic poems as he was for his embodiment of the Romantic values. The phrase "Byronic hero" is still used today both to describe Byron and the heroes of his poems like "Don Juan." The Byronic hero is idealized but flawed—a man of great talent, passion, and privilege. He also often has a distaste for his own privilege in a way that only the privileged can afford to have. He almost always has a tragic past, and almost always meets a tragic end. Basically, he was what every man devoted to the Romantic movement wanted to be.

Byron had an enormous passion for everything in life, and his relationship with his dog Boatswain was no exception.

Lord Byron inherited his family estate, Newstead Abbey, when he was only ten years old, which gave him his title, a large amount of land, debt, and probably a huge ego boost from becoming a lord before he could legally drive. Boatswain joined the household in 1803, when Byron was fifteen. Though he was called a Newfoundland, the life-sized portrait of him hanging in Newstead makes him look like more of a husky-Newfoundland mix.

From the start, the poet and the puppy were inseparable. Byron, who was an avid swimmer, enjoyed throwing himself out of boats pretending to drown just to see if Boatswain would come to his rescue, presumably to create a viral video (but really, that Internet fad from a few years back where people would pretend to faint in front of their dogs to see how they'd react is nothing new). Byron was, unsurprisingly, not a very responsible dog owner (he was not super responsible at anything) and let Boatswain run free, playing with the aforementioned tamed bear and wreaking havoc around the estate grounds. In a particularly notorious incident, he jumped through an open window and onto a tea party being hosted at Newstead. Byron also once used Boatswain to trash the room of a guest at their estate with whom he was feuding. Byron's childhood friend Elizabeth Pigot illustrated cartoons featuring Byron and Boatswain's exploits and published them in a children's book called *The Wonderful History of Lord Byron and His Dog.*

Boatswain met his end when he was bit by a rabid dog and contracted rabies himself. Byron was devastated and nursed him by hand to the end, even though he likely knew the dangers of exposure to the disease. He was with Boatswain until he crossed the rainbow bridge.

Byron was so devastated over the death of Boatswain that he had a huge monument erected in his honor on the grounds of Newstead, in spite of his aforementioned enormous debt. The monument was built in the ruins of the Abbey itself, close to where the altar would have stood, which is a very Byron thing to do. The monument was the only building work that Byron ever carried out during his time at Newstead Abbey, because he had other things to do, like be a fake military general, spend money he didn't have, and be bisexual. The tomb is engraved with a poem written by Byron and friend John Cam Hobhouse. Three years later, still in mourning, Byron wrote in his will a request that his final resting place be alongside Boatswain, beneath the "Epitaph for a Dog."

In the end, Boatswain's tomb was bigger than Byron's.

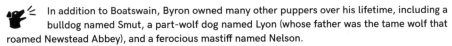

sidebark

 In addition to Boatswain, Byron owned many other puppers over his lifetime, including a bulldog named Smut, a part-wolf dog named Lyon (whose father was the tame wolf that roamed Newstead Abbey), and a ferocious mastiff named Nelson.

Another famous Newfoundland owner/writer was J. M. Barrie, whose dog Luath was the inspiration for Nana, the dog nanny in Barrie's most famous work, *Peter Pan*.

THE BROWN DOG AFFAIR

Or, JFC Let's Stop Experimenting on Dogs

MUTT · ENGLAND · 1800s

Warning: This story is horrifying and includes a lot of humans being complete dicks to animals. It's also about the beginning of the end of testing on animals, so there's a positive message. But if you can't handle it—no worries. Just skip to the next good boi.

The TL;DR is that humans are sometimes asses to dogs, whom we don't deserve.

Our story starts in Victorian England. The thing you need to know about Victorian England is that it was the actual worst. Because cholera and no rights for anyone but rich white men and sewage everywhere and too many people and fashion that would literally kill you if you wore it. And you'd better hope you never got a cold, broke a bone, had a kid, lost a tooth, or stubbed your toe because literally any of those things could kill you. And if they didn't, the doctors trying to cure you of said ailments could kill you with their treatments. And it would be a painful death because no anesthesia.

Lots of scientists were working to try and make this better. The understanding of anatomy and the human body was improving, and medical research was becoming more complex and accurate. The only problem was that most of these scientists thought

the best way to conduct their research was through vivisection.

What is vivisection? It's dissection but worse because the thing you're cutting up is alive. And usually that thing was an animal.

I KNOW—IT IS THE WORST. Stay with me.

People were calling them on this straight-up nonsense. In 1875, the National Anti-Vivisection Society was founded by a badass lady named Frances Power Cobbe, who spent her whole life campaigning for things like women's rights and against things like cruelty to animals. At the time, there were about three hundred experiments on live animals happening every year in London, often in professional institutions. Through the work of Frances and other activists, the Cruelty to Animals Act was passed in 1876, which set limits on the practice of animal experimentation and instituted a licensing system.

It was only kind of a good thing. Limits are a good first step, but animal experimentation wasn't outlawed entirely. Instead, the law required that experiments could only be done on anesthetized animals that would then be killed as soon as the experiment was over. It also required licensing for vivisections, but many of those licenses were granted in secret, or overlooked thanks to a well-placed bribe.

(Imagine me saying this in my most deadpan, King-George-in-*Hamilton* voice:) Awesome. Wow.

As the Victorian era became the Edwardian, nothing really improved. No one was following the rules that had been laid down in 1876, and few were being punished for it. Let's talk about two examples: first, Ernest Starling, professor of physiology at University College London, and his brother-in-law William Bayliss; and second, Ivan Pavlov.

Yeah, *that* Pavlov! Turns out he was a super dick! Let's start with him.

We remember Pavlov's experiments as being the discovery of the conditioned reflex after Pavlov observed that his dogs salivated at the sound of the bell that accompanied their feeding.

Let's unpack that.

So, first of all, they weren't his dogs. They were lab dogs. And they were in the lab because they were being used for experiments. Rather than experiment on an animal once then kill it as the kind-of-not-great law required, Pavlov kept his dogs alive and continued to subject them to brutal experiments until it killed them.

Second, his research was not initially psychological. Pavlov's early work focused on ways in which eating excited salivary, gastric, and pancreatic secretions. To do that, he developed a system of "sham"-feeding dogs: He would remove their esophagi and create an opening in each dog's throat so that the food would fall out and never make it to the stomach, then observe how this affected their secretions. This HORRIFYING

research won him the 1904 Nobel Prize in Physiology or Medicine, which makes me want to flip a table.

Later, Pavlov did start to focus his research on "psychic secretions": drool produced by anything other than direct exposure to food. "Right," you say, "the bell!" Wrong. The bell wasn't what made the dogs salivate: It was the sight of the lab coats that Pavlov and his assistants wore when they were about to feed the dogs whose esophagi had been removed.

Hold on, I have to go throw up and then hold my puppy close and promise I will never let anything bad ever happen to her.

So, on to our second story of how humans are the worst. The aforementioned Starling and Bayliss wanted to pick up Pavlov's research by using vivisection on dogs to determine whether the nervous system controlled pancreatic secretions. Bayliss had a license to practice vivisection, but he wasn't following the rules. He was operating on the same small brown terrier dog over and over again. In February 1903, Starling opened up the dog's abdomen to inspect the result of an earlier operation, then made a completely new wound in the neck for the purpose of a demonstration to students. After the lecture, the dog was killed. The professors claimed the dog was properly anesthetized, but the audience said otherwise and claimed the dog was howling in pain the whole time.

Among those audience members were two badass anti-vivisectionists who were there undercover as students in order to blow the whistle on Bayliss and Starling. The two women, Louise "Lizzy" Lind-af-Hageby and Leisa K. Schartau later published *The Shambles of Science: Extracts from the*

Diary of Two Students of Physiology, which included the story of the cruelty they had seen toward the brown dog. The book came to the attention of Stephen Coleridge, honorary secretary of the National Anti-Vivisection Society, who then brought a libel suit against Bayliss and Starling.

Coleridge lost the suit, but the publicity surrounding the trial was enough to draw many allies to the anti-vivisectionist cause and galvanized the movement. Eventually, the experiment, trial, and resulting outrage became known as the Brown Dog Affair.

In one of the most dramatic gestures to come out of this, a monument to the brown dog erected in London and funded by an anonymous donor. The statue bore this inscription:

In Memory of the Brown Terrier Dog done to death in the Laboratories of University College in February, 1903, after having endured vivisection extending over more than two months and having been handed over from one Vivisector to another till death came to his release. Also in memory of the 232 dogs vivisected in the same place during the year 1902. Men and women of England, how long shall these things be?

Basically, it's a much more badass and far less problematic version of *Three Billboards Outside Ebbing, Missouri*, and hell yes, I would watch *One Monument in the GD Middle of London*.

When the monument went up, the medical community freaked out. Students and professors rioted in protest of this slander against their research, and petitioned to get the statue removed. Some even tried to pull it down themselves but were stopped by police. Medical and veterinary students marched from Trafalgar Square to King's College in protest. They were met by the anti-vivisectionists, and riots broke out, called the Brown Dog Riots. They continued throughout the month of December in 1907.

The statue was eventually removed, simply because it was more trouble than it was worth, but the anti-vivisection movement continued throughout the twentieth century. Groups like Britain's National Anti-Vivisection Society kept the cause alive, and increasingly strict rules were enforced on animal testing, though many animals still suffer in the name of human science.

In 1985, a new version of the Brown Dog statue was placed in Battersea Park. It bears the same inscription as the original, although the actual dog statue is different. He commemorates the suffering of millions of animal test subjects throughout history and today.

GREYFRIARS BOBBY

And Other Loyal Dog Tails

SKYE TERRER · SCOTLAND · 1850s

Our culture is full of stories of loyal dogs. From *Homeward Bound*, the movie that traumatized me as a child, to the Twitter photos of dogs lying next to the coffins of fallen soldiers that will literally always make me cry (literally. always.), to the way our hearts swell when our own dogs go absolutely berserk when we walk in the door after a day at the office. One of the best things about our doggos is just how h*ckin' loyal they are.

One of history's most loyal dogs is a Scottish Skye terrier known as Greyfriars Bobby.

Few actual facts can be definitively attached to the legend of Greyfriars Bobby. Enough sources from the time corroborate that a little dog lived in the churchyard in Edinburgh, but who he belonged to and why he was there vary with the telling. The most likely candidate for Bobby's human, based on burial records and Edinburgh censuses, was a gardener named John Gray. When John Gray and his family moved to Edinburgh in 1850, he joined the police as a night watchman to avoid the workhouse. Each night on his rounds, he was accompanied by his Skye terrier, Bobby.

Skye terriers are one of the only terrier breeds today whose appearance has stayed the same since they were first recorded in the sixteenth century. The dogs can be recognized by their distinctive long coat (usually cut with lustrous bangs, making them the Zooey Deschanel of dogs), short, sturdy legs, and tall ears. In Johannes Caius's *Of Englishe Dogges*, one of the first books on dogs written in 1570, the Skye is described as "brought out of barbarous borders from the uttermost countryes Northward . . . which, by reason of the length of [hair] makes showe neither of face nor of body." Though most dogs have changed considerably because of breeding over the centuries, the Skyes are still pretty true to that original description.

Skye terriers hail from the Isle of Skye in the upper Scottish Hebrides, where they were used to protect livestock from burrowing animals like badgers, foxes, and weasels. Their longs coats helped protect them from bites from those animals. Today, they're considered an endangered breed by the AKC—only thirty were born in the UK in 2005, and only forty-two were registered in 2012—but they were popular as both working dogs and companions in the 1800s.

When John Gray died in 1858, he was buried in Greyfriars Kirkyard (which is

Scottish for "churchyard"). And after so many nights walking the streets together, side by side, Bobby decided that even in death, his place was by his master.

According to legend, Bobby spent the next fourteen years living in the cemetery where Gray was buried, sleeping at his master's grave. At the one-o'clock gun from the Edinburgh Castle every afternoon, he would leave the churchyard for a meal at the coffeehouse he used to frequent with Gray. The cemetery groundskeeper initially tried to drive him away, but relented when Bobby proved himself a useful resident—he would kill rats and fight off the cats and occasional schoolboys who came into the churchyard with the intent of making mischief.

News of the dog loyal even in death spread, and tourists started to come to Edinburgh just to see Bobby. He was written up in papers all over the country, and artists came to sketch him.

In 1867, a law was passed that required all dogs in the city to be licensed or they would be killed. Which was not great for Bobby because it's hard to buy your dog a license if you're dead. Luckily, Sir William Chambers, the lord provost of Edinburgh, paid Bobby's license and gave him a collar with the inscription "Greyfriars Bobby from the Lord Provost 1867 licensed." The collar is now on display at the Museum of Edinburgh.

For fourteen years, Bobby kept constant watch over Gray's grave, until he died in 1872. He was buried near the entrance of the Greyfriars Kirkyard, near John Gray. Bobby's headstone reads, "Greyfriars Bobby – died 14th January 1872 – aged 16 years – Let his loyalty and devotion be a lesson to us all."

When Baroness Angela Georgina Burdett-Coutts, president of the Ladies' Committee of the Royal Society for the Prevention of Cruelty to Animals, heard about the life and death of Bobby, she was so moved by his story that she asked for permission to erect a monument to the dog in Edinburgh. She commissioned sculptor William Brodie to create a bronze likeness of Bobby to be placed on top of a granite fountain on Candlemaker Row, opposite Greyfriars Kirkyard. The statue is still there, and you can give Bobby's nose a rub for good luck—it's turned shiny and gold from all the dog lovers from around the world who have come to give him a good scritch.

NEWS OF THE DOG LOYAL EVEN IN DEATH SPREAD, AND TOURISTS STARTED TO COME TO EDINBURGH JUST TO SEE BOBBY. HE WAS WRITTEN UP IN PAPERS ALL OVER THE COUNTRY, AND ARTISTS CAME TO SKETCH HIM.

Bobby is one of many, many dog-at-his-master's-grave stories that make up dog lore around the world. The Ancient Greeks told the story of Eupolis, a poet whose dog was so attached to him he died of starvation on his master's tomb. The Romans had the story of Theodorus, a man whose dog grieved on his coffin. In the 1700s, a story was passed around Scotland that a greyhound was walking ten miles each night to sleep on its master's grave. When Paris passed an ordinance prohibiting dogs from cemeteries, people protested that this would just make things worse for the hordes of grieving dogs whose stories kept showing up in the papers. Stockholm has a story of Fidele, who lived in the Maria Cemetery in the center of the city, keeping vigil on his master's grave. Rose Hill Cemetery in Maryland has a statue of Rollo, a faithful dog. Montana has a story about a dog who refused to leave the railway station from which his master's coffin departed for burial. Hachikō, Japan's most famous dog, continued to go to the train station where he met his master every day for years after his master's death.

Basically, if, like me, you google "dog at master's grave stories," you will find 73,700,000 results, half of which are stories and half of which are fact-checkers debunking these stories.

Whatever the truth about Greyfriars Bobby—or any of these dogs—I think it's pretty clear that the bond between human and canine goes both ways.

sidebark

 Skye terriers play an important role in British history. Sir Edwin Landseer, the artist best known for his lion sculptures in Trafalgar Square, produced many paintings of Skye terriers. They were also some of Queen Victoria's favorite dogs, which hugely increased their popularity during the Victorian era in England, when small dogs were the go-to accessories for the upper classes.

 Skye terriers have gone by many names over the years, including the Clydesdale terrier, the fancy Skye terrier, the silky Skye terrier, the Glasgow terrier, and the paisley terrier.

SEMPER FIDO

How "Fido" Became Synonymous with "Dog"

MUTT · UNITED STATES · 1850s

What's the long German word for when something gets so popular it then becomes unpopular but still remains relevant in the cultural lexicon?

Because that's what happened to Fido. In spite of the name being almost synonymous with "dog," Fido doesn't even crack the Internet's top one hundred most popular dog names these days. And yet, if you say "Fido" to anyone, they know exactly what kind of animal you're talking about.

So where did it all start? Who was the OG Fido?

The name itself is a variation on the Latin word *fidelis*, which means "to trust or put faith in." Calling your dog Fido is the equivalent of calling him Trusty or Faithful, which makes sense because loyalty is one of the characteristics we most prize in our dogs.

So whose Fido was the Fido that paved the way for all other Fidos?

Good old Abraham Lincoln.

Before he was president, Lincoln was a lawyer in Springfield, Illinois, with a menagerie of a house. His family owned several dogs and cats, the most famous of which was Fido, a yellow mutt with floppy ears and a stubby tail.

Fido was a favorite dog of both the Lincolns and Springfield. Lincoln and Fido would walk to town each day, and Fido was known to patiently wait outside the barber shop while his hooman got his haircut. When Lincoln had a package to carry, he'd often give it to Fido to hold in his mouth. In the evenings, Fido would be fed table scraps and romp on the living room rug with Lincoln and his sons. Lincoln's law partner William Herndon wrote that "if exhausted from severe and long-continued thought . . . [Lincoln] would get down with a little dog . . . to recover." A profile of Fido published in *Life* magazine in 1954 called him a "frisky mongrel," which is my new Twitter bio.

As Lincoln prepared to take up his place in the White House, one thing became clear: Fido may have been the pet of a president, but he wasn't a presidential pet. When Lincoln's victory was announced with fireworks and cannons, Fido was terrified and hid under the family couch. The throngs of people stopping by the Lincoln home to visit and congratulate the president elect similarly stressed Fido the fork out.

So Lincoln made the very tough decision to leave Fido in Springfield in the care of a local carpenter, John Roll, who had two sons around the same age of the Lincoln boys. His adoption came with a long set of rules for the care and keeping of Fido: Fido was never to be tied up outside. He was not allowed to come indoors when he scratched at the door. He must be allowed to wander freely about the table as the family dined and was to be given scraps. He was never to be chided for muddy paws in the house. Though all the Lincolns' furniture was sold or auctioned off before their move, Abe made sure that a special couch stayed with the Rolls, because it was Fido's favorite to sleep on.

He even had Fido's formal portrait taken to travel with him and his family to the White House. Mass media was just starting to take hold of the country, and photography was a fairly new technology (sidebar—how did anyone get their dog to stay still long enough for an old-time photo, and how much peanut butter was involved?). The public, already obsessed with their new president-elect, became similarly obsessed with Fido. His photo was printed in news-papers around the country, which is when

THE NAME ITSELF IS A VARIATION ON THE LATIN WORD *FIDELIS*, WHICH MEANS "TO TRUST OR PUT FAITH IN." CALLING YOUR DOG FIDO IS THE EQUIVALENT OF CALLING HIM TRUSTY OR FAITHFUL.

the name Fido skyrocketed in popularity. It continued to top the charts throughout Lincoln's presidency and then came back strong again after his assassination in trib-ute. As mourners flocked to Springfield for the president's funeral, Fido was taken back to Lincoln's home there, and mourners were able to meet the dog. For many who were deeply affected by Lincoln's death, Fido was a small part of their president left behind.

ADOPT DON'T SHOP!

Caroline Earle White Founds America's First Animal Shelters

UNITED STATES · 1833–1916

It seems like every other video on my Twitter feed is a heartwarming story of a shelter dog whose life was changed after its adoption. BTW, this isn't a complaint. I will 100 percent watch every one of them, and 100 percent of them will make me cry because so many good dogs finding good humans and together making good homes is what my heart is made of. And as someone who grew up with and adored a cast of damaged shelter dogs, adoption is what made me a dog person.

But without the work of Caroline Earle White, my heart would be significantly less warmed, because we wouldn't have the dog shelters, humane societies, and animal rescue organizations that fill our feeds today.

Caroline Earle White was born in Philadelphia in 1833 to Quaker parents. Both were abolitionists, and her mother was cousin to famous suffragette Lucretia Mott and was involved in the movement herself. So Caroline grew up in a family of woke social justice warriors.

In 1856, Caroline married Richard White, a wealthy attorney who would eventually introduce her to Henry Bergh, a New York businessman who, in 1866, formed the American Society for the Prevention of Cruelty to Animals. However, their main focus was protecting horses, because horses were considered valuable property.

Inspired by his work, Caroline decided to do the same in her hometown of Philadelphia. She teamed up with another local animal rights activist, Colonel M. Richards Muckle, to start an organization similar to Bergh's. But when the Philadelphia Society for the Prevention of Cruelty to Animals was formed, Richard White, Caroline's husband, and Colonel Muckle were among the board members.

Caroline, its chief architect, was not.

BECAUSE HISTORY IS A SEXIST SON OF A BITCH. I feel like I already wrote this book . . .

So Caroline started a splinter group of the PSPCA—the Women's PSPCA, or the Women's Humane Society, as it was known. This was a common practice at the time. Women were often instrumental in social justice movements of the day but barred from leadership positions within those movements, so they would form these splinter groups that were women-only. That way they could be in charge and get sh*t done.

Caroline and her group took up the cause of getting stray dogs off the streets of Philadelphia. In the mid-nineteenth century, cats were more typically indoor animals, used to keep down the rodent population. Dogs were used for work in cities—typically as watchdogs—and even dogs that were pets were usually allowed to run free through the town. This resulted in a lot of unplanned dog pregnancies, and contributed to the spread of rabies. The Women's Humane Society raised funds to create a facility to give refuge to stray dogs. It became the first animal shelter in the nation. The refuge was located in Bensalem, Pennsylvania, about twenty miles northeast of downtown Philadelphia. Prior to that, unwanted animals, particularly stray dogs who could spread rabies, were rounded up and killed by municipal employees.

Caroline's shelter was the first to introduce the country to the ideas of humane animal sheltering and adoption, and imitators quickly sprang up. The Women's Humane Society expanded from rescuing dogs off the street to also taking them in from dog-fighting and -baiting rings. They raised money for more water fountains in cities, hoping both that animals would benefit from more convenient access to water and that more access to water would encourage men to drink less booze—most of these women were also big into temperance. They also fought for laws governing the transporting of horses and against sports like fox hunting.

Caroline's cause took on another angle when a scientist contacted her asking for any stray dogs they rescued to be sent his way for medical testing. She was HORRIFIED and not only refused but also founded the American Anti-Vivisection Society (see: the Brown Dog Affair in this very book). The society was the first of its kind in America, and branches were soon started around the country.

The Humane Society Caroline founded still operates today.

---

sidebark

Much like today, most of the dogs found in early shelters were mutts, but the way people thought about these mixes was very different. If you were rich enough to have a dog as a pet in the nineteenth century, you wanted to be sure it was a *purebred*. Mutts, or mongrels, were considered a subpar species. People were even warned of the dangers of keeping mongrels as pets. A warning pamphlet included the advice "No one would plant weeds in a window box or a flower garden. Why have mongrels as pets?"

"HELLO?
YES, THIS IS DOG"

*How Alexander Graham Bell's Dog
Helped Invent the Telephone*

SKYE TERRIER · SCOTLAND · 1847–1922

Before Alexander Graham Bell invented the telephone, the iron lung, hydrofoil, modern metal detectors, and a host of other things, he tried to teach his dog to talk.

In fact, without that talking dog, we may not have the telephone at all.

Alexander was born in Edinburgh, Scotland, in 1847. When he was around twelve, his mother began to go deaf. Alexander found the best way to communicate with her was by speaking close her forehead so she could feel the vibrations of his voice. His father, a renowned elocutionist, also devised a system of transcribing words and vocalizations into symbols representing the shape and movement the lips and tongue formed to make them. These two things led young Alex to explore how the "visible speech" method could help deaf people communicate vocally despite having never heard how the words they were saying sounded, simply by showing them how to move their mouths.

He began his experiments on his Skye terrier, Trouve.

The first task was to teach Trouve to growl on command, then to do it while standing on his hind legs so that Alexander could more easily reach and manipulate his mouth. Using the training from his father's method, Alexander would shape Trouve's mouth to produce the sound *ma, ma, ma* from his growl. In time, and with a lot of treats, Alexander's dog was able to pronounce "Mama" in a humanlike way all on his own with the combination of growling and lip moving. Alexander added new syllables to Trouve's vocabulary—*ga*, *ah*, *ow*, and *oo*. By arranging these sounds, Alexander successfully taught his dog to say "How are you, Grandmama?" Having proved his theory on his dog, he went on to introduce this method to several students he worked with at a school for the deaf.

In 1873, Alexander became a professor of vocal physiology at Boston University, where he met his future wife, Mabel Hubbard, who had completely lost her hearing to scarlet fever. Living and working with the hearing-impaired sparked Alex's interest in the principles of acoustics and experiments in transmitting sound waves over wires, which would lead to his invention of the telephone. He also opened his own school for the deaf, and the wealthy parents of two of the students he helped teach to speak were so impressed that they decided to help financially support his inventing.

However, it's all a little more complicated than this (the tagline of history). In spite of his work, Alexander's motivations for developing this communication method were

ALEXANDER SUCCESSFULLY TAUGHT HIS DOG TO SAY "HOW ARE YOU, GRANDMAMA?"

based in a growing movement of the time to eradicate sign language and deaf culture. In 1880, a large, multicountry convention called the Second International Congress on the Education of the Deaf, or shortened to the Milan Conference, was held. The conference passed several resolutions confirming that lipreading should be the preferred method for the deaf to communicate with hearing individuals, and that sign language should be discouraged or even banned. Those in favor of oral communication exclusively were called oralists (*resists urge to make inappropriate joke*). So, sure, Alexander helped Helen Keller learn how to speak,

and, sure, he worked with deaf kids that society had basically written off, but also he supported eugenics, and thought the deaf shouldn't be allowed to reproduce. So. His heart might have been in the right place—just like the delegates of the Milan Conference, he believed his work was beneficial to the deaf community. Doesn't mean it wasn't still problematic af.

As a result of this, many deaf people who couldn't read lips couldn't communicate. Deaf professionals lost their jobs—particularly teachers who had previously communicated with their students through and taught sign language—and there was a general decline in the deaf in the labor force because of difficulty communicating with hearing counterparts. Deaf students were beaten for using sign language in school and had their hands tied behind their backs to prevent them from signing. The quality of life for the deaf decreased dramatically. In response, the National Association of the Deaf was founded in the United States, which promoted sign language preservation and deaf rights.

Since the Milan Conference, oralism and sign language have begun to coexist more peacefully, but it wasn't until 1970 that sign language was recognized as an official language.

Miles to go before we sleep.

THEY SEE ME ROLLIN'

Bud Nelson and the First Cross-Country
Road Trip in the United States

PIT BULL · UNITED STATES · 1903

It's *Mad Max: Furry Road*! Cruising down the barely there highways of turn-of-the-century America is Bud Nelson, the pit bull who donned a pair of custom goggles and became the copilot on the first cross-country automobile trip.

1903—Cars were still new, dangerous, and difficult to drive. Many people weren't convinced they'd ever truly replace the horse and carriage. Cars were loud. They raised huge clouds of dust. They were unreliable. England had passed a law that when driven, cars had to have someone walk in front of them with a red flag warning pedestrians, cyclists, and carriages of the oncoming danger. Which sort of defeats the purpose. Tennessee required motorists to post a week's notice before they undertook a trip anywhere in an automobile. Also, purpose: defeated.

By the beginning of the twentieth century, there were only eight thousand automobiles in the United States—compared with fourteen million horses.

Within a decade, everything would be different.

Change began with a bar debate in the fancy University Club of San Francisco about which was better, the car or the carriage. A guest named Horatio Nelson Jackson was the lone dissenting voice in favor of the horseless carriage and made a case for its sticking power. The debate soon turned to an argument, then a wager, and in a scene straight out of *Around the World in 80 Days*, someone bet that Horatio couldn't make it to New York City in less than ninety days by automobile. The wager was fifty dollars.

Horatio accepted, though he didn't know much about cars. He was a thirty-one-year-old former doctor who had given up his practice after being diagnosed with tuberculosis. His interest in automobiles was mostly a hobby, so he decided to find a professional to help him with his cross-country drive. He invited Sewall Crocker, a twenty-two-year-old bicycle racer and gasoline engine mechanic, to join him on the trip. Together, they acquired a twenty-horsepower gasoline-powered cherry-red Winton touring car that Horatio named Vermont after his home state. Cars at the time weren't cheap—in today's money, you'd have to shell out a minimum of around thirty thousand dollars for one—or easy to operate, but Horatio had an inherited fortune and the confidence of a straight white man in 1900s America! They were ready to go!

Now all they needed was a dog to stick its head out the window.

Four days after the bet, on May 23, 1903, Horatio and Seawall started their engine and lurched their way out of San Francisco and onto the road. They would be traveling four thousand miles to New York City, though there were only 150 miles of paved roads in the whole United States—most in cities.

On day nineteen, the two reached Idaho, a trip that today would take about thirteen hours. While stopped, a man offered to sell Horatio a blond pit bull for fifteen bucks. Horatio said yes, and when they left Idaho, Bud the dog was the Chewbacca of this motley crew. Bud loved motoring. He sat in the front seat of the car and watched the road. To prevent the huge amounts of dust kicked up by the vehicle from damaging his eyes, Horatio got him a custom-made pair of goggles—or, as I like to call them, doggles.

Horatio hoped that Bud might be a good-luck charm for their journey. He wasn't. A good boy, yes, but good luck, not so much. The trip was plagued with bad luck, bad directions, and bad decisions. Horatio later said that Bud was the only one of the crew who never used profanity on the road. Several times, Vermont had to be towed by a team of horses, the most ironic form of AAA roadside assistance ever. They were lost in the Badlands for thirty-six hours. Had to wait five days for a replacement part when a connecting rod snapped. Their gas tank sprung a leak, and Seawell had to bike twenty-six miles to the nearest town for help. They were all three thrown from the car in an accident.

But our intrepid trio continued on, undaunted, and soon their trip was the talk of the nation. Press began to wait for their arrival in each town, and by the time they reached Omaha, cheering crowds greeted them. Bud was by far the most photogenic and popular (and fashionable, because doggles) of the three.

Sixty-three days, forty-five hundred miles, and eight thousand dollars (about two hundred thousand in today's cash) later, Vermont, Seawall, Horatio, and Bud rolled into Manhattan on July 26 at four-thirty A.M.

The real kicker? Horatio never got the fifty dollars he originally bet.

But the first great American road trip was complete.

sidebark

Pit bulls' bad reputation for being vicious fighting dogs likely traces back to their origins in England, where they were bred first as fighters for the absolutely gross sport of bear- and bullbaiting, then used in a sport called *ratting*, where a bunch of rats were put in a pit and dogs would compete to see who could kill the most. Gross, gross, gross, gross, gross. But pit bulls aren't bred to be vicious—they're bred to be strong and intelligent, and their stereotypical ferocity is often a result of how they're treated by the bad humans around them, not something rotten in their nature. Pit bulls are, in fact, often gentle and great family dogs. In a dog behavioral test performed by the American Temperament Test Society, pit bulls placed second with an 83.4 percent pass rate, beat out only by the Labrador retriever.

LIZZIE BORDEN TOOK AN AX...

... and Used It to Chop Up Treats for Her Boston Terriers

BOSTON TERRIER · UNITED STATES · 1860–1927

In 1892, in the small town of Fall River, Massachusetts, Lizzie Borden supposedly took an axe and gave her stepmother forty whacks and gave her father forty-one.

Though in reality, it was closer to twenty-nine whacks total, and Lizzie was found innocent of the murders, but that just doesn't roll off the tongue quite as well.

Lizzie grew up in an affluent family, though her father couldn't quite shake the habits from his impoverished childhood of scrimping and saving. So in spite of having plenty of money, the Borden house had no indoor plumbing or electricity. They lived very sparsely because of their strict religion.

After Lizzie's mother, Sarah, died, her father Andrew married a woman named Abby Gray. And Lizzie wasn't saying she was a gold digger . . . but she was pretty sure Abby only married her father for his money.

Tensions were high in the Borden household in the days leading up to the murders, though no one is quite sure what exactly was going on behind closed doors. As a result, no one has ever been able to come up with a definitive motive for why Lizzie might have killed her parents. She may have been upset not only by the presence of her new stepmom, but also that her father was gifting large sums of money to Abby's family when he couldn't even be bothered to invest in a bathroom that didn't require going outside. Her father had also recently killed some of Lizzie's pet pigeons—maybe that sent her over the edge. There's also speculation that Lizzie was physically and possibly sexually abused by her father, or that her own sexuality and the stress of being a closeted queer woman in the 1800s made her prone to snap.

But all we can do is guess. Because we just don't know.

What we do know is that around eleven A.M. on August 4, Lizzie called out to the family's maid, Bridget Sullivan, that she had found her father dead.

Under the headline SHOCKING CRIME!: A VENERABLE CITIZEN AND HIS AGED WIFE HACKED TO PIECES IN THEIR HOME (side note—aged wife? LOL, okay, she was sixty-four and he was sixty-nine, but whatever, journalism lives by the sexist double standard), the *Fall River Herald* sent the town and the nation into a frenzy. Hundreds of townspeople visited the crime scene, trampling any evidence into nothing.

Two days after the murder, papers began reporting evidence that Lizzie might have had something to do with her parents' deaths. A clerk at S. R. Smith's drugstore in Fall River told police that Lizzie visited the store the day before the murder and attempted to purchase prussic acid, a deadly poison. In a super-weird twist,

SHE WAS DOG MOM TO THREE BOSTON TERRIERS, NAMED ROYAL NELSON, DONALD STUART, AND LADDIE MILLER. THEY DIDN'T CARE THAT LIZZIE WAS POSSIBLY A MURDERESS AND/OR ONE OF THE MOST MALIGNED WOMEN IN AMERICA. A BELLY RUB IS A BELLY RUB IS A BELLY RUB.

in the days leading up to the murder, the whole household had terrible food poisoning, though Abby had suspected it was actual poison. The police were baffled by the lack of blood anywhere but on the bodies and no discernible murder weapon, but they were suspicious of the fact that Lizzie had been home the whole time and not seen a murderer—in spite of the fact that, according to forensic evidence at the time, Abby was killed almost ninety minutes before Andrew. She also had the most to gain from his death—when he died, Andrew Borden was worth almost ten million dollars in today's money, and Lizzie and Emma inherited a significant portion of that.

When Lizzie was questioned, she was confused and couldn't keep her story straight. No one considered that she was grieving the loss of her father, had witnessed something tragic and probably scarring, and also had been given morphine to help her nerves, all of which may have affected her mental faculties.

After a highly sensationalized and publicized trial, Lizzie was acquitted by a jury of twelve men, each more mustachioed than the last. Lizzie's was one of the first trials in American history that was covered by mainstream media and magazines in the same way modern murder cases like the Amanda Knox trial are publicized today. Like many of those cases, at its center was what American society deems an unlikely murderer—a prim, affluent white woman.

Life after acquittal was difficult for Lizzie. Though she was able to purchase an enormous house in the nice part of town, all of her friends abandoned her. People refused to sit near her at church. Children would dare one another to ring her doorbell in the middle of the night. Strangers would pelt her house with gravel and eggs. She also became estranged with her sister, Emma, over Lizzie's relationship (yes, *that* kind of relationship) with an actress named Nance O'Neil.

But Lizzie found comfort in dogs.

Lizzie developed a fondness for blackand-white Boston bull terriers—a fashionable breed among the New England upper class at the time—and often had one with her when she took chauffeur-driven rides in the country. She was dog mom to three Boston terriers, named Royal Nelson, Donald

Stuart, and Laddie Miller. They didn't care that Lizzie was possibly a murderess and/or one of the most maligned women in America. A belly rub is a belly rub is a belly rub.

Boston terriers were a relatively new breed at the time. During the 1870s, breeders in Boston developed them by crossing an English bulldog and the white English terrier. The breed was originally known as the Round-Headed Bull and Terrier, but in 1891 was renamed Boston terrier in honor of its birthplace. It was one of the first American breeds recognized by the AKC, and is considered a "modern" dog because it was bred exclusively for companionship.

In 1913, Lizzie helped fund a rescue center in her hometown of Fall River to care for abused draft horses, and in 1917 helped again when it expanded its mission to dogs and cats. In her will, drawn up just before she died in 1927, Lizzie wrote, "To the Animal Rescue League of said Fall River the sum of thirty thousand dollars, also my shares of stock in the Stevens Manufacturing Company. I have been fond of animals and their need is great and there are so few who care for them."

Today, the Animal Rescue League still receives funds from Lizzie's trust.

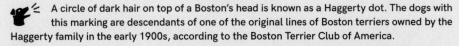

sidebark

 A circle of dark hair on top of a Boston's head is known as a Haggerty dot. The dogs with this marking are descendants of one of the original lines of Boston terriers owned by the Haggerty family in the early 1900s, according to the Boston Terrier Club of America.

In 1728, Boston banned dogs higher than ten inches because stray dogs were stealing meat from street vendors. LOL, okay, don't you know the little ones are the craftiest?

NATIONAL BARK RANGER

John Muir and Stickeen, Partners in Adventure

SMALL BLACK MUTT · ALASKA · 1909

John Muir was many things. Naturalist. Adventurer. Writer. Sierra Club founder. Professional tramp. National park preserver. Kick-ass beard haver.

John was born in Scotland in 1838 but raised in Wisconsin. His life changed when, at age thirty-one, he was nearly blinded by an industrial accident at the wagon wheel factory where he worked. After four weeks recovering his sight, he decided to refocus his life and devote himself to learning everything he could about the natural world. He quit his job and became a self-proclaimed professional tramp, walking all over the country before finding his heart in Yosemite National Park in California. Muir's evocative and transportive writings about Yosemite inspired more visitors to come to the park and gave him a platform to preach conservation. One of his most famous articles, "In God's First Temples: How Shall We Preserve Our Forests?" called for California legislators to take a stand against the depletion of Yosemite caused by livestock and deforestation. In 1890, Yosemite was declared an official national park and thus protected land.

Let's go back about a decade: In 1880, John Muir joined Reverend S. H. Young on an exploration of the icy southeast region of Alaska, particularly Glacier Bay. Along for the ride (literal ride because they were in canoes) was the reverend's dog, Stickeen. John was not crazy about Stickeen being part of their crew. He also was generally not crazy about Stickeen, which, in turn, makes me not crazy about John Muir. Stickeen was small, and John told the reverend that the journey would be too hard for him. But the reverend refused to be separated from his pupper, and Stickeen was officially initiated into their pack.

Unlike most other dogs on adventuring crews, such as the previously recounted Seaman the Newf, Stickeen didn't really have a job on the trip. He wasn't a working dog. He didn't pull sleds or protect the crew or help with hunting. His favorite thing to do was lie quietly in the bottom of the canoes until they started drawing close to the shore, at which point he would take a flying leap into the freezing water and swim the rest of the way. Just to be an independent sassypants. When their camp was packed up each morning and the canoes ready to be pushed off, Stickeen would never come when they called—probably because he knew they wouldn't leave him behind and wanted to fully milk the situation. Even when they faked paddling away, he took his sweet time getting to the canoes. Muir wrote, "He seemed to meet danger and hardships without anything like reason, insisted on having his own way, never obeyed an order, and the hunter could never set him on anything, or make him fetch the birds he shot."

WHEN STICKEEN MADE IT ACROSS THE BRIDGE, JOHN REACHED DOWN TO LIFT HIM UP THE REST OF THE WAY, BUT STICKEEN WAS SO PROUD HE LAUNCHED HIMSELF UP ONTO THE GLACIER AND BEGAN HIS OWN CELEBRATORY SURVIVAL DANCE PARTY. JOHN WROTE, "NEVER BEFORE OR SINCE HAVE I SEEN ANYTHING LIKE SO PASSIONATE A REVULSION FROM THE DEPTHS OF DESPAIR TO EXULTANT, TRIUMPHANT, UNCONTROLLABLE JOY."

This dog had an attitude, and I love it.

One morning, when John set out alone to explore a glacier during a blizzard (sure, John. Great idea), Stickeen decided to follow him. Together they hiked until they came upon a crevasse that was too wide to leap. To get across, they would have to climb down into the crevasse, cross over on a sliver of ice that served as a quasi bridge, then climb back up.

Which did Stickeen a frighten. The previously unfazed dog was suddenly very fazed and absolutely, positively refused to cross.

And, for the first time, John felt his heart melt a little toward the dog. John later wrote, "His looks and tones of voice when he began to complain and speak his fears were so human that I unconsciously talked to him in sympathy as I would to a frightened boy." John went first, but it took a long time to get Stickeen to follow him. John tried to lure him along the path he had already made, to encourage him, even to pretend he was going to walk away and this was Stickeen's last chance to come along. Nothing worked. The snow was rising and the light was going out, and the pair were running out of time to get back to camp.

John was ready to walk away.

But then Stickeen made his leap of faith. He put his two front feet together and slid down to the first foothold John had made, then down to the bridge.

When Stickeen made it across the bridge, John reached down to lift him up the rest of the way, but Stickeen was so proud he launched himself up onto the glacier and began his own celebratory survival dance party. John wrote, "Never before or since have I seen anything like so passionate a revulsion from the depths of despair to exultant, triumphant, uncontrollable joy."

The two made it back safely to camp, and the previously independent and single-minded doggo refused to leave John's side for the rest of the trip. They were trauma bonded, and John said that every time he and Stickeen would make eye contact, he felt like Stickeen was saying, "Hey, remember that time we almost DIED on a glacier? Good times, man."

"I have known many dogs," John later wrote, "and many a story I could tell of their wisdom and devotion; but to none do I owe so much as to Stickeen."

All these quotes come from John's story "Stickeen: The Story of a Dog," which was first published in the *Century Illustrated Monthly Magazine* but has been adapted and reprinted over and over. It became one of John's best-known works and is considered one of American literature's classic dog stories.

John Muir went on to do some of his most important work for conservation, including partnering with President Teddy Roosevelt, my historical boyfriend, and founding the Sierra Club, which fought and continues to fight for the protection of the natural world, but he never forgot Stickeen, even after the doggo had crossed the rainbow ice bridge to dog heaven, where all glaciers are navigable and no crevasses need be crossed.

AND THE PAWSCAR GOES TO . . .

Dogs in the Movies

UNITED STATES · 20TH CENTURY

As long as there have been films, there have been dogs saving babies or traveling long distances to find their people or drooling all over Tom Hanks while solving crimes on the silver screen.

There's some debate as to who the first dog to appear in film was, since so many silent films have been lost to time. One of the first we know of was Blair, a British collie, who appeared in a six-and-a-half-minute film released in 1905 called *Rescued by Rover*. The film, about a heroic collie saving a baby, was directed by Blair's owner, and starred the owner's daughter as the rescued baby, so who says nepotism isn't alive and well? The film became so popular and so many prints were made that the negatives wore out, causing the director to reshoot the entire film twice to keep up with demand. A sequel was soon made, and Blair, stage name Rover, was a bone-a-fied star. (And yes, this film is what popularized the dog name Rover!)

In 1910, Laurence Trimble, an aspiring writer and actor, visited the motion picture company Vitagraph Studios to research a story he was writing about filmmaking. He brought along his collie named Jean. While on the set of the newest film, the director happened to need a dog actor. And since she was there, Laurence suggested Jean. Right place, right time, girl. Turns out, she was a natural, and went on to star in dozens of films, many directed by Laurence. Jean not only became the first dog to have a leading role in motion pictures in the US, she was the first dog to have her name in the title of her films.

As more films were made, and more dogs cast in them, a cottage industry of animal actor trainers started to spring up too. Carl Spitz ran one of the most successful, the Hollywood Dog Training School. Their most prestigious alumnus was Terry, a purebred Cairn terrier, who was dropped off for training by her owners and then never picked up (maybe had something do with the Great Depression and dogs being expensive—just a hunch). Carl ended up keeping Terry, and eventually got her cast in *Bright Eyes*, a 1934 picture with Shirley Temple. It was up to Shirley herself to decide which of the called-back dogs got the part, and she picked Terry because Terry and Shirley's Pomeranian, Ching-Ching, hit it off.

Another actress who took an immediate

liking to Terry was Judy Garland, which led to her being cast as Toto in *The Wizard of Oz*.

The role was demanding for a little pupper. Terry's stunts included being put in a basket, withstanding wind machines mimicking a tornado, and jumping across a closing drawbridge. She rose to every task. Her only fault? According to Judy's daughter Lorna Luft, Judy reported that Terry had terrible breath, making it hard to not wince when the dog would pant in her face. Terry was paid $125 a week, more than many of the human actors in the film. Judy was so in love with Terry she offered to buy her from Carl Spitz when the film wrapped.

The Wizard of Oz changed film history with its use of Technicolor. Terry became an instant star, beginning with her walking the red carpet at the film's premiere at Grauman's Chinese Theatre in 1939. Since she was called Toto by all her fans, Spitz felt it was only right to officially change her name.

Some dog stars came from more humble beginnings than Hollywood's most elite dog-star-making school. Higgins, a mutt born in 1957, was adopted from the Burbank Animal Shelter by trainer Frank Inn. Inn later told reporters that Higgins was the smartest dog he had ever worked with. Higgins had an expressive face and was able to convey many emotions, and could master tricks like yawning and sneezing on cue. Higgins had a successful run in TV and film before he was cast in the movie that would define his career: *Benji*. When the word spread that the beloved star of *Benji* was rescued from a shelter, the number of adoptions from the American Humane Society spiked. When Higgins died at eighteen years old, his daughter Benjean took over the role of Benji in three additional movies.

Another dog star came from an unlikely beginning on the battlefields of World War I. In 1918, while serving abroad in France, American corporal Leland Duncan discovered a German shepherd with five young puppies in a bombed-out German encampment. Duncan took them back to his barracks, where they were adopted by the other soldiers in his platoon. Duncan kept one of the puppies and named him Rin Tin Tin.

When World War I ended, Duncan took Rinty (adorable nickname is adorable) back to America with him and began training him to do a variety of tricks, including clearing a twelve-foot hurdle. Once Rinty was trained, Duncan took him to Poverty Row, a strip in Hollywood where small B-movie studio offices were located, and started knocking on doors. This got Rinty a small part in a melodrama called *The Man from Hell's River*, and shortly afterward he was given a starring role in *Where the North Begins*. The film was a huge success, and Rin Tin Tin became a celebrity. He went on to make twenty-three films.

Warner Bros. got thousands of fan letters for Rinty, each of which was returned with a photo of Rin Tin Tin autographed with a paw print. Rinty's films were so profitable that Warner Bros. paid him almost eight times as much as they paid human actors. He was known as the mortgage lifter because every time the studio was hurting financially, it would release a Rin Tin Tin film and the books would balance. According to Hollywood legend, Rin Tin Tin received the most votes for Best Actor at the first Academy Awards in 1929. He was removed from the competition because the Academy thought it more appropriate to have a human winner receive their first statuette.

Another of Hollywood's most famous dogs was Pal. At two years old, Pal's trainer, Rudd Weatherwax, took the dog to MGM to audition for an upcoming film called *Lassie Come Home*. Based on the popular 1940 novel by Eric Knight, *Lassie* was the story of a loyal collie who struggles across hundreds of miles of English countryside to rejoin the boy she loves.

TWIST! Pal didn't get the part! Instead the role went to a show dog, and Pal was the understudy.

But in a story straight out of *42nd Street*, when Pal stepped in to do a stunt involving crossing a river that the show dog couldn't do, director Fred Wilcox proclaimed Pal was the real Lassie and immediately fired the show dog. He even reshot the scenes from the first six weeks they'd spent working on the film—this time with Pal as the star. The movie was released in 1943 and became an enormous hit. Pal went on to star in six more Lassie films, as well as pilots for the *Lassie* television series. When the TV show was picked up, Pal was too old to play the part, but Lassie Junior, Pal's son and stand-in, took over the role. The show ran for nineteen years, and all the dogs used to portray Lassie were descendants of Pal.

In 1960, Lassie/Pal/all the Pals and Rin Tin Tin were honored with stars on the Hollywood Walk of Fame. The other ultimate pavement memorial for actors, handprints outside of Grauman's Chinese Theatre, has gone to only one dog—Uggie, the Jack Russell terrier that starred in *The Artist*, which won Best Picture in 2011. Uggie arrived at the theater in a fire truck, and after pressing his paw prints into the cement, was given a fire hydrant–shaped cake (which seems like it could have been a recipe for disastrous confusion).

Canines in Hollywood have a long, storied history—this short glimpse is in no way comprehensive, but the fictional characters they played are some of the most iconic of all time.

Like the saying goes, if you can bark here, you can bark anywhere.

---

sidebark

Like all things in Hollywood, animal acting has a dark side. Many animals, including dogs, have been hurt, endangered, or even killed for film. There was so much public outcry when a horse broke its spine after being ridden off a seventy-foot cliff during the filming of *Jesse James* in 1939 that American Humane was tasked with overseeing the treatment of animals on Hollywood sets. Today, American Humane works in association with the American film and television industry to help ensure the well-being of animal actors while on set, and awards the "No Animals Were Harmed" seal to films that pass their standards. However, there's still often little done to monitor the living conditions or working hours of animal stars. We've come a long way but still have a long way to go.

MY BARK WILL GO ON

Dogs on the Titanic

ATLANTIC OCEAN · 1912

We know there were twelve dogs on board the *Titanic*.

We also know there may have been more.

The dogs on board the *Titanic* were listed as cargo in the ship's records, and many of those specific cargo details have been lost, because, you know. It's the *Titanic*.

The dogs brought aboard the luxury ocean liner were the pets of men like John Jacob Astor, the most privileged white male passenger on a ship of privileged white people. The *Titanic* was very dog friendly—the ship's carpenter, John Hutchinson, was responsible for taking care of the dogs in their large kennels on deck F. Several toy dogs were kept in the first-class cabins with their people, though technically this was against the rules—turns out there are no rules when you're super forking rich and on the *Titanic*. The kenneled dogs were exercised daily on the poop deck (every deck is a poop deck when there's a dog on it, amirite?) by a steward or one of the bellboys. There was even a dog show planned for April 15.

Obviously, that didn't happen.

We've all seen the movie. We all had a weird fascination with disasters as a child. We all know that at 2:20 A.M. on April 15, 1912, the *Titanic*, unsinkable ocean liner, struck an iceberg and sank.

Why was the *Titanic* considered unsinkable? It spanned 883 feet from stern to bow, and its hull was divided into sixteen compartments that were presumed to be watertight. Because four of these compartments could be flooded without causing a loss of buoyancy, the *Titanic* was given its infamously ironic moniker.

When it hit the iceberg, five of those compartments were ruptured. Which I guess no one thought could possibly happen.

The *Titanic* was a high-tech marvel of the turn-of-the-century world. It had elevators! Wireless communication! Telephones! They couldn't call the shore, but still! Telephones! It was built at a time when the goal was to make everything faster, bigger, and stronger. More regulated was not on the list of priorities, which is why there were fewer lifeboats than passengers. In the aftermath of the sinking, rules were adopted requiring that every ship have lifeboat space for each person on board, and that lifeboat drills be held. An International Ice Patrol was also established to monitor icebergs in the North Atlantic shipping lanes; it required ships to maintain a twenty-four-hour radio watch.

The sinking of the *Titanic* was one of the first large-scale disasters resulting from man-made error, and since it happened to a lot of rich people, everyone cared about it a lot more than about all the poor people who were dying en masse in factories at the same time. The effects spanned the globe. Only seven hundred of the twenty-two hundred passengers on board survived, and people from every continent (except Antarctica, obvs) died.

THERE WAS ROOM ON THAT DOOR FOR AT LEAST ONE MORE DOG.

The three dogs that survived the sinking of the unsinkable ship had one thing in common: They were small enough to fit comfortably aboard a lap on a lifeboat. Of course, my St. Bernard is pretty sure she fits comfortably on my lap, but these dogs were all small—one Pekingese and two Pomeranians, both breeds with an average weight of under fifteen pounds. One of the Pomeranians, named Lady, was in the cabin with her mistress, Margaret Hays, when the order was given to evacuate. Miss Hays wrapped Lady in a blanket and carried her with her to the lifeboats. The second Pomeranian was owned by a family named the Rothschilds.

The Pekingese was named Sun Yat-Sen. He belonged to Henry and Myra Harper, heirs to the company that would become Harper-Collins Publishers (*waves to my fiction editor at Harper*). They also brought Sun Yat-Sen on the lifeboat with them, and, when asked about this decision, Henry said, "There

seemed to be lots of room, and nobody made any objection." LOL, sure, Jan.

Among the dogs that didn't survive the sinking were a Cavalier King Charles spaniel, an Airedale terrier named Kitty (who belonged to J. J. Astor), a toy poodle, a fox terrier, a French bulldog (a champion named Gamin de Pycombe, who had just been purchased for the modern equivalent of around fifteen thousand dollars), and a Great Dane. The owner of the Great Dane, Ann Elizabeth Isham, refused a spot in a lifeboat when she was told she would have to leave her dog behind, and she died with him (me as a dog owner on the *Titanic*).

Aside from the human inclination to be fascinated with disaster, why is it that we are *still* obsessed with the *Titanic*? Why not the French ship *Mont-Blanc*, which exploded in Halifax Harbour in 1917? Or the *Eastland*, which capsized in the Chicago River so fast that no one was able to board the way-too-many lifeboats that were weighing it down? Or even the *Lusitania*, which was torpedoed during World War I and is partially responsible for launching US involvement in the war? There are a lot of theories, and a lot of factors. One, because it happened to rich people and celebrities, and it is a truth universally acknowledged that everyone cares more about things that happen to rich people. But it also happened to a wide variety of people, forming a sort of microsociety in those more than two thousand passengers on board. The mixing of people in disaster foreshadowed a breakdown of the traditional American class system post–World War I.

Second, it happened in exactly the right way, which is a strange thing to say about a disaster. It happened in a concentrated amount of time, rather than spread out nebulously across several days, like the Great Chicago Fire a few years earlier, or too fast, like the *Eastland*. And because it happened to so many people on a not-too-large and also not-too-small scale, it gives opportunities for individual experience and choice within the disaster, which heightens the drama. It's also loaded with dramatic irony—the greatest technological achievement of its day felled by an iceberg. No matter how advanced we get, man bows to nature.

Whatever the case, I think we can all agree—there was room on that door for at least one more dog.

sidebark

Passenger Charles Moore was planning to transport one hundred English foxhounds on the *Titanic*, but changed his mind at the last minute, THANK GOODNESS.

There's a well-worn tale of a Newfoundland named Rigel who belonged to First Officer William Murdoch being aboard the *Titanic*. As the rescue boat *Carpathia* approached, Rigel was able to bark loud enough that the ship's captain could locate the lifeboats. FALSE—the story is a myth. There is no record of William Murdoch having a dog on board, and even a well-insulated water dog like a Newfoundland would have had a hard time surviving for that long in freezing waters.

James Cameron was far from the first to monetize a tragedy for cinematic success. Just weeks after the sinking, actress Dorothy Gibson, who had survived the disaster, starred in a film about it, proudly touting that she was wearing the same coat in the film she'd actually been wearing the night the *Titanic* sank. The sinking also inspired poems, books, and songs—112 pieces of music inspired by the sinking were copyrighted in America in 1912 alone.

A SMALL HISTORY OF THERAPY DOGS

How Does That Make You Feel?

CHOW CHOW AND YORKIE · 20TH CENTURY

Animal-assisted therapy traces its roots all the way back to Ancient Greece, where horses were used to lift the spirits of the severely ill. In the ninth century, a hospital farm in Gheel, Belgium, included working with farm animals as part of the treatments for their patients. In the late 1700s, the York Retreat, an asylum in England, was the first to document the use of animals with the mentally disabled, as they encouraged the residents to work on the property farm. Florence Nightingale observed that small pets reduced the levels of anxiety and stress in psychiatric patients, which began a wave of informal experiments involving animal interaction with humans to produce a calming effect.

The most famous therapy dog belonged, fittingly, to history's most famous therapist: Sigmund Freud. Freud was late to get on the dog bandwagon: He was seventy when his daughter Anna brought home a German shepherd named Wolf, and Freud fell in love—so much so that his daughter stopped giving him birthday presents and instead just gave him pictures of Wolf. When Freud got his own dog, a chow chow named Jofi, the father of psychoanalysis gained not only a companion, but an office assistant.

The first patient Jofi provided comfort for was Freud himself. By this point in his life, Freud had cancer of the jaw, which resulted in painful surgeries, prosthesis, and difficulty chewing and speaking. While going through a series of operations and hospital stays, Freud wrote to a friend, "I wish you could have seen with me what sympathy Jofi shows me during these hellish days, as if she understood everything."

It wasn't long before Jofi started joining Freud for sessions with patients, and he quickly noticed a change. Freud not only observed the calming affect Jofi could have on his patients, but also how in tune she was to human emotions, and started taking cues about the mental state of his patients from Jofi. She would lie near a patient if they were depressed and needed comfort, whereas she would keep her distance if the patient was anxious. Freud also noticed that children in particular seemed better able to disclose painful information with a dog nearby, though many adults were similarly affected. Jofi's presence lowered the barriers humans put up to avoid talking about painful subjects.

Jofi also had a finely tuned internal clock as to when a session was over—a hint clients didn't always get from Freud himself. Because of his painful cancer, any sessions over an hour were difficult for him, so at exactly fifty minutes, Jofi would get up, stretch, and head for the door, letting the patient know that it was time to wrap things up.

After Jofi, the first official therapy dog was a four-pound Yorkshire terrier that was found by American soldiers in New Guinea during World War II. She was purchased for $6.44 by Bill Wynne, a twenty-two-year-old corporal from Ohio, from a fellow soldier who had found her underfed in a foxhole. Wynne named her Smoky, and over the next several years, the pair would survive air raids, typhoons, and twelve combat missions together.

Smoky's ability to serve as a therapy dog first manifested when Wynne caught dengue fever and was sent to the hospital. His friends brought Smoky to see him, and the nurses were so charmed by her they asked if they could bring her around to visit with other wounded soldiers. During the five days Wynne spent in the hospital, Smoky slept with Wynne on his bed at night, and in the morning, the nurses would collect her to take her along on patient rounds.

The idea of taking a dog on hospital rounds led Elaine Smith, an American nurse, to start a program where dogs were allowed to visit patients in hospital in 1976. Her organization, Therapy Dogs International, began with six dogs—five German shepherds and one collie. As of 2012, when the most recent numbers were made available, TDI has grown to twenty-four thousand registered dog/handler teams, and is one of many therapy dog organizations around the world. The American Kennel Club even offers therapy dog certification. While Elaine started out using her dogs only in hospitals, therapy dogs can now be seen at assisted living centers, elementary schools, disaster relief sites, hospices, libraries, homeless shelters, courtrooms, and funeral homes. Even without the certification required to be an official therapy dog, studies show that any interaction with a dog can lower blood pressure. Petting a dog releases the stress-reducing hormone oxytocin and decreases the production of the stress-causing hormone cortisol. Dog contact has also been linked to reduced cholesterol and decreased triglyceride levels, which contribute to better cardiovascular health.

So go pet a dog—it's good for you.

sidebark

What's the difference between a therapy dog and service dog? Service dogs are trained to perform tasks and to do work that eases their handlers' disabilities. Therapy dogs also receive training, but their responsibilities are to provide psychological or physiological therapy to individuals other than their handlers. Despite thorough training, registration, and the therapeutic benefits therapy dogs provide, they do not have the same jobs or legal designation as service dogs. Therapy dog handlers don't have the same rights to be accompanied by their dogs in places where pets are not permitted. Though there are laws preventing businesses from demanding to see service dog registration, remember—it's super unethical to try and pass off your dog as a service dog (or an emotional support dog) to get it special privileges. Don't make your pup complicit in your crime!

THE DOGS OF WAR, PART I

The Canine Combatants of World War I

EUROPE · 1914–1918

Trench warfare sucks.

Let's be honest—war in general definitely sucks, but it's considerably worse when you're fighting ankle-deep in a foul combination of standing water, decaying corpses, and human waste. Not to mention the fact that you're staring down your enemy in an almost perpetual stalemate across a barren, treacherous no-man's-land, waiting to see which of you will attempt a suicide charge first.

And yet that's the way humans have decided to fight many of their wars.

Probably the most famous site of trench warfare was the Western Front of World War I, a four-hundred-plus-mile stretch of land through France and Belgium that saw some of the war's most crucial and brutal battles. In spite of the fact that World War I was a global conflict, the trenches of the Western Front are some of the most remembered battlegrounds not only of that war, but in history.

Trench warfare also doesn't lend itself to super-effective communication among battalions. Along the Western Front, dogs were crucial in getting messages between companies when other means of

communication had been knocked out. Human messengers were easy targets, but dogs were small, hard to spot, and much more difficult to take out.

One of the most legendary messenger dogs of World War I was a black mutt named Satan, who had a huge impact on the outcome of the Siege of Verdun, one of the longest and most savage conflicts of the war. It lasted almost eleven months, the longest battle in modern history, and, for the Germans, the main purpose was to wipe out as many French troops as possible before the British could reach them. Verdun was an important city historically to the French, and the Germans had picked it because they knew that losing it would crush the morale of the people and the soldiers.

The French troops were struggling to hold Verdun. Communication was down, and there was no way to know where reinforcements were—or if they were coming at all. They were running out of food and ammunition. Back at HQ, French commanders were desperately trying to get a message to the trapped soldiers that help was coming if they could just hold on a little longer, and to get coordinates from them to

plan their attack. Seven men were killed trying to deliver the news, and carrier pigeons couldn't get past the German snipers.

Finally, Satan was chosen—partly because he was fast and fearless and black, which was helpful for moving at night, and partly because his handler, a man named Duvalle, was one of the trapped soldiers in Verdun, and they knew Satan would find him. With a gas mask, a message tucked into his collar, and two carrier pigeons in baskets on his sides, Satan took off toward Verdun.

The French soldiers saw him coming, an ironically named savior from the other side. But as quickly as they got their hopes up, the Germans spotted Satan too, and he was shot in the leg. Satan staggered and then fell.

But Duvalle had already recognized his dog, and when he saw him fall, he climbed out of the trench and reportedly shouted, "Satan, my friend!" (Again, irony.) "Have courage!" Duvalle was instantly gunned down by sniper fire, but hearing his voice was all Satan needed—miraculously, he dragged himself to his feet and managed to run the rest of the way to the trench, where he delivered the message that had been stashed in a metal tube in his collar: *For God's sake, hold on. We will relieve you tomorrow.* In reply, the captain wrote the coordinates for the location of the German gun battery on two notes, which were sent with the pigeons Satan had brought. One was shot, but the other made it back to HQ, and a few hours later, French reinforcements were able to not only launch a counterattack, but hold on to Verdun in what would be the beginning of the end for the Germans.

In addition to messengers, dogs were used to transport equipment, as sentries,

and as company mascots on both sides. They were not only essential parts of the war effort, but also essential psychological support and comfort for the soldiers, and helped distribute one of the most important stress relievers for men in the trenches: cigarettes. Serving in the trenches made war, which is already pretty rough, even more stressful, and an important form of self-care that helped soldiers calm down was smoking. Remember—this was back when people thought tobacco was healthy for you. Health aside, tobacco was an effective way to calm nerves on the battlefield, and cigarettes were effective tobacco delivery systems that stayed lit and weren't as cumbersome as a pipe or cigars.

DOGS WERE USED TO TRANSPORT EQUIPMENT, AS SENTRIES, AND AS COMPANY MASCOTS ON BOTH SIDES. THEY WERE NOT ONLY ESSENTIAL PARTS OF THE WAR EFFORT, BUT ALSO ESSENTIAL PSYCHOLOGICAL SUPPORT AND COMFORT FOR THE SOLDIERS.

The YMCA, Salvation Army, and the Red Cross (which should tell you something about how little was known about how bad smoking really was for you) all distributed cigarettes to the troops in the trenches, and soon discovered the most effective way to do so was by strapping them to the backs of dogs. The dogs would then run through the trenches, delivering cartons of cigarettes to soldiers and probably also getting scratches on the head. These dogs were usually small terriers, though French bulldogs and Boston terriers were also used. The terriers also helped keep the rat population down. The poor sanitary conditions in the trenches attracted rats (some of which were as big as cats, so hello to my nightmare) and other disease-carrying trash pandas, but terriers would catch and kill them.

Dogs were also trained to find wounded men on the battlefields after a firefight. They had to make their searches at night and alone. When they found a wounded soldier, they were trained not to bark, since that could draw enemy fire. Instead, they would pull a piece of the soldier's uniform off and bring it back to their handler, who would then leash them and dispatch a rescue attempt for the wounded soldier. They also carried medical packs they would leave with the soldiers so they could treat themselves. Some dogs even stayed with dying soldiers until they passed to comfort them. Airedales and bloodhounds were best for this work.

There were around ten thousand of these Red Cross dogs used during World War I, and they saved thousands of lives. 15/10 all.

sidebark

 I would be remiss if I didn't mention one of the most famous individual dogs to serve in World War I, Sergeant Stubby, a stray mutt rescued on the Yale University campus by 102nd Infantry Regiment and smuggled to the front lines when they were deployed. He became the company's official mascot, and served for eighteen months and participated in seventeen battles on the Western Front. He warned his regiment of mustard gas attacks, found and comforted the wounded, and once caught a German soldier by the seat of his pants and took him hostage. Stubby was one of the most decorated dogs of World War I, and the only dog to be nominated for rank and then promoted to sergeant through combat—though it was likely just a ceremonial title. Whatever the case, he looked adorable with all those little medals.

The word *terrier* comes from the Latin word *terra*, meaning "earth," because terriers would follow burrowing animals into their holes to catch them.

RUSSIA'S LAST ROYAL DOGS

Although the Tsar Did Not Survive,
One Dogter May Be Still Alive

SPANIEL · RUSSIA · 1918

In spite of a certain animated movie whose soundtrack I may be listening to at this very moment, Princess Anastasia didn't survive the execution of her royal family, the Romanovs.

However, one member of the royal household did.

The Romanovs were the second dynasty to rule Russia. They were established in the 1600s, and after five generations of leadership, they were pretty sure they were blessed by God. The Romanovs ruled as absolute monarchs, meaning that they believed they had been appointed by the big man Himself, and as a result, they could do whatever they wanted and were subjected to no checks and no balances.

Tsar Nicholas II was not only the last of the Romanov dynasty *and* the last tsar of Russia, he was also the most legitimately terrible. Not because he was a bad guy necessarily—he was just hugely underprepared to be in charge of one of history's most massive countries. You would think that, if one is next in line for the throne, one would get a little bit of schooling on how to run an empire. But Nicholas's father was sure he was going to live forever. Or at least longer than he did. So when he

died unexpectedly, Nicholas was twenty-four and had a law degree, a hipster beard, and no training to be a tsar. He also had absolutely no desire to be in charge: When he was a child, he was traumatized when his grandfather, who was tsar at the time, was assassinated in front of the whole family.

And now the job was his! Hard pass.

Nicholas was überconservative and extremely nonprogressive at a time when Russia desperately needed some progress. There was no parliament, no constitution, none of the infrastructure needed to support rapid industrialization, food shortages, and an enormous, mostly impoverished population growing increasingly unhappy about the upper tiers of society living large while they were literally eating dirt to survive.

But they did have a brutal secret police. *finger guns*

This rapid industrialization was creating the perfect breeding ground for communism, a political school of thought based on the writings of Karl Marx, which, to grossly oversimplify, believes that means of production should be owned collectively by all and social classes should be abolished.

The first indication that Russia was in desperate need of some leadership was when they lost the Russo-Japanese War in 1904. Russia, which is the size of forty-five Japans, should not have lost that war. When people rose up in protest of what an embarrassing loss it had been, Nicholas panicked and murdered them all. The day became known as Bloody Sunday. Around one hundred people were killed and thousands more injured.

Things got worse when World War I broke out. Because of strong alliances with France, Nicholas went to war against Germany (though the kaiser was his cousin—royal inbreeding is fun!). So on top of having nothing to eat, the population of Russia was now being shipped off to a war they wanted nothing to do with.

Which is when Nicholas got a great idea. What if . . . and stay with me here . . . in spite of not knowing anything about military leadership . . . what if . . . *he* was in charge of the army? Because being grossly underprepared for a position had never stopped him before.

Everyone: "Nicholas, no."

Nicholas: "NICHOLAS, YES."

I am not sure why he thought this was a good idea—literally everyone advised against it—but he took up control of the Russian army. Which meant that every defeat was now blamed directly on Nicholas. And there were lots of defeats.

To make things worse, Nicholas left his wife in charge of the government back home, and you know me, I would never say that women are incapable of running a country, but this woman was. Tsarina Alexandra was as good at leading Russia as her husband was at leading its army. Her rule destabilized the government until it basically fell apart. Food shortages increased, the death toll on the Western Front continued to rise, and Alexandra reacted by tightening her grip on government control, leaning hard into her conservativism, and hiring and then firing ministers with no warning and no reason (sound familiar? Time is a flat circle, y'all). Her chief advisor was Rasputin, an illiterate self-proclaimed faith healer who way overstayed his welcome after he "healed" the Romanovs' son, Alexei. Rasputin went on to give Alexandra a lot of terrible advice, and was eventually assassinated in 1916 (multiple times—we all know this story, right? If you don't, put down this book and google that sh*t right now. It. Is. Bananas.).

Segway—let's talk about the Romanov kids! Nicholas and Alexandra had four daughters and a lot of panic, because everyone knows girls can't inherit an empire! There was, if we're doing it like the Spice Girls, Olga, the romantic, Tatiana, the boss, Maria, the ingénue, and Anastasia, the spitfire.

Finally, in 1904, the tsar and tsarina welcomed a tsarevich—Alexei Romanov. Awesome! Penises are so essential for emperorship! Except for one thing—Alexei had a disease called hemophilia, which caused his blood to not clot, so even a paper cut could cause him to bleed out. Alexandra and Nicholas did everything they could to help their kid, but mostly they focused on keeping his disease secret from the Russian public so as not to give them any more reason to doubt their leaders. (Spoiler alert: They had plenty of other reasons.)

All five of the Romanov children were animal lovers, and kept cats and dogs at the palace. The three dogs we're going to talk about the most are Ortipo, a French bulldog that belonged to Tatiana; Anastasia's

Cavalier King Charles spaniel, Jimmy; and Alexei's cocker spaniel, Joy.

Joy was a descendant of a cocker spaniel brought from Great Britain and became inseparable with Alexei: He took the dog with him on holidays and trips. Nicholas sometimes took his son to the front lines of World War I to support the morale of the troops and strengthen Alexei's patriotism because the battlefield is not at all traumatizing for a child, and Alexei al ways brought Joy. Great, sure, super-fun outing for your preteen son and his dog.

So World War I was going terribly. Russia wanted out, but Tsar Nicholas, who you remember is supreme leader appointed by God and hands everyone who challenges him a note that says *I do what I want*, refused to back out. Food shortages on the home front led to more protests, which Nicholas attempted to quell with the army. Turns out the army was also hungry and joined the protests.

There was only one thing to do: In 1917, Nicholas abdicated the throne, and he and his family were taken into custody.

Nicholas stepping down made it possible for exiled communists like our good friend Lenin to return to Russia. Lenin immediately got to work undermining the provisional government that had been established after Nicholas's abdication and starting his own rival government, known as the Petrograd Soviet, which was made up of men from his communist faction called the Bolsheviks.

After peaceful Bolshevik protests turned violent when the army opened fire on them, Lenin decided it was time for revolution, and this time, it was personal. And also violent. The Bolsheviks seized the Winter Palace, the seat of the Russian government.

Initially, this seemed like it could be great: Lenin called for a whole bunch of fun things, like an end to Russian involvement in World War I, the abolishment of private landownership, the introduction of a minimum wage, increased rights for women, universal health care, and free elections. It was the last one that bit him in the ass, because the problem with free elections is that when you let the people choose, they don't always choose you, and in 1917, the Bolsheviks lost the election. Lenin immediately ordered his men to shut down the elected assembly and placed himself in charge instead. Cool, cool, cool . . . what could go wrong?

Russia finally managed to pull out of the War in 1918, but it resulted in a lot of their territory going to Germany and the Austro-Hungarian Empire. Not everyone was happy about this, and many enemy factions of the Bolsheviks joined together to take them out, thereby kicking off the Russian Civil War. The Bolsheviks were known as the Reds. Everyone who opposed them were known as the Whites. The Whites included people who supported the tsar, liberals, conservatives, supporters of the Allied powers—absolutely anyone who wasn't a Bolshevik. And we know that only a Sith deals in absolutes.

Initially, the revolution went great for the Whites. They were supported by the Allies and managed to take control of most of the former Russian Empire, executing millions of Reds along the way. However, the area they captured was a lot of Siberia and farms and wasteland. Meanwhile, the Bolsheviks held on to all the industrialized, heavily populated cities with lots of infrastructure, which were far more useful for a militant revolution.

But as a White capture of the city of Yekaterinburg was beginning to look imminent, the

Bolsheviks started to get nervous. Yekaterinburg was important because it was where Tsar Nicholas and his family were being held in exile in Ipatiev House, and there were enough Tsar supporters among the Whites that, if they got him back, there was a chance they'd make him their leader again. And we all saw how that went before.

Rather than turn the former Tsar over to the Whites, the Reds decided the best thing to do would be to assassinate him and his whole family. Real chill-like.

On the night of July 16, 1918, the Romanov family was told they were being taken to the basement of their prison home for their protection, as the Whites were marching on Yekaterinburg and they were in danger. Once they got to the basement—surprise! Their execution orders were read to them, and the soldiers opened fire. Despite what certain animated movies/hit Broadway musicals might have told you, Nicholas and Alexandra, as well as the five children, were all killed. Another casualty was Anastasia's dog, Jimmy, who she had brought with her. She was holding him when the soldiers fired. Ortipo, Tatiana's Frenchie, was also killed for barking too much in the yard.

But what about Joy? Dear, bewildered Joy.

I found conflicting reports. I read that he had grown prone to wander since the family came to Yekaterinburg and wasn't at the house when the family was executed. Another article suggested he *was* in the basement with the Romanovs but hid during the executions and managed to escape when the bodies were carried out. Whatever the case, he made it, the sole survivor of the imperial family.

When the Whites captured Yekaterinburg, White officer Pavel Rodzyanko spotted a stray dog in the street and recognized him as Alexei's dog, Joy—Joy was a celebrity dog in Russia and had appeared on postcards and in photos with the royal family—and took him in. When Rodzyanko fled to the UK after the Whites were forced to retreat and the Bolsheviks won the Revolution, Joy went with him and was given as a gift to King George V, who was a cousin of Nicholas II. Joy was given a place in the English court and lived out the rest of his life there.

Baroness Sophie Buxhoeveden, a former lady-in-waiting to the tsarina who made it out of St. Petersburg and met Joy when he was with Rodzyanko, wrote in her autobiography, "What had little Joy seen on that terrible night of July 16? He had been with the Imperial Family to the last. Had he witnessed the tragedy? His brain had evidently kept the memory of a great shock, and his heart was broken. . . . Little Joy was well cared for. He . . . spent the last years in the utmost canine comfort, but still never recovered his spirits." He was buried in Windsor Gardens under a small headstone with the unintentionally poignant inscription "Here lies Joy."

sidebark

Ortipo the Frenchie was a gift to Tatiana in one of history's great love stories. While working as a nurse in World War I, she met a wounded soldier named Dimitri, and THEY FELL IN LOVE AS SHE NURSED HIM BACK TO HEALTH. I mean, the novel writes itself. He later gave her Ortipo as a token of his affection, and Tatiana wrote in her diary, "The dog is overly cute," which is also something I posted on Instagram about my dog today. Royals—they're just like us!

THE WAR OF THE STRAY DOG

Or, the Curious Incident of the Dog in the War-time

MUTT · GREECE · 1925

It's happened to every dog owner: You're on a walk, or at the dog park, and your dog is being totally calm and normal and then suddenly they take off at a full-blown run for no reason, and you chase after them screaming, "Come back!" And they reply, "H*ck you, Karen!" or possibly, "SQUIRREL!"

However, this usually this doesn't result in a firefight, an international incident, and a mini war.

But that's what happened in 1925 in the Incident at Petrich, or, as it's better known, the War of the Stray Dog.

Greece and Bulgaria already weren't friends. They'd been bickering over territory for years, and Greece was sure Bulgaria was bankrolling the Macedonian independence movement, which Greece was not into because they wanted Macedonia to stay un-independent and theirs. And because they shared a border, peasants from both sides would run over into the other country and raid property. Which no one was into. They had already fought the Second Balkans War over territory, which was brought to an abrupt halt when the world decided it had bigger problems, namely World War I.

The Bulgarians had allied themselves with the wrong side in World War I and were forced to give up land as a result. So they were already crabby when a Greek soldier's dog saw probably a ball or something and took off at a full run. His master, of course, chased him. Right over the Bulgarian border.

WE DON'T KNOW WHAT HAPPENED TO THAT STRAY DOG. BUT WE DO KNOW THAT THE CONFLICT HE STARTED WILL GO DOWN IN HISTORY AS ONE OF THE STUPIDEST, YET MOST INSTAGRAMMABLE, WARS EVER.

Which Bulgarian troops took as a great excuse to open fire, killing the soldier, as well as a Greek captain and his aid who walked into no-man's-land with a flag of surrender to try and cool things down.

This wasn't the first time skirmishes had broken out at the border, but it was enough to send Greece's president, Lieutenant General Theodoros Pangalos, over the edge. Pangalos had won his position through a coup, and he was eager to prove just how legit he was as a ruler. He decided to make an example of the skirmish of the stray dog and demand reparations. Pangalos was already the worst—as president, he suspended freedom of the press, devalued Greek currency by literally cutting paper notes in half, and even dictated how long women's skirts should be. So it's no surprise he was looking for an excuse to throw a fit.

Bulgaria apologized and proposed an investigation. Not good enough, said General Pangalos. What he wanted instead was two million francs to compensate the victims' families. Then he presumably finished the phone call by saying "You have forty-eight hours," and hanging up dramatically like the Bond villain he was.

When Bulgaria refused, Greece said, "We warned you." Then they invaded Bulgaria, specifically the city of Petrich, and managed to set up an occupation there. Bulgaria ran to the League of Nations, aka Europe's mom, which stepped in and demanded Greece stop it and pay Bulgaria an apology fee. Greece had no choice but to agree.

Pangalos was humiliated, and this defeat was part of the reason he was overthrown the following year and replaced by the president *he* had overthrown. How embarrassing.

We don't know what happened to that stray dog. But we do know that the conflict he started will go down in history as one of the stupidest, yet most Instagrammable, wars ever.

DIRE WOLVES AGAINST DIPHTHERIA

Togo, Balto, and the Great Race of Mercy to Save Nome, Alaska

HUSKIES · ALASKA · 1925

We open on: Nome, Alaska, 1925—a small, remote town in the middle of winter.

Cut to interior, where a broadcaster sits before a radio, frantically signaling. Snow can be heard gusting outside, and drifts pile up against the windows.

Radio operator: "Nome calling . . . Nome calling . . . We have an outbreak of diphtheria . . . No serum . . . urgently need help . . . Nome calling . . . Nome calling . . ."

Shockingly, this isn't the intro of a zombie apocalypse horror film. It's the setup for the Great Race of Mercy to save a small Alaskan town from a pandemic. Just not of the zombie variety.

Nome was a gold rush town, though by 1925, when our story begins, most of the gold was gone. The previously booming population of twenty thousand in 1900 had shrunk to around fourteen hundred by 1925. One-third of that population was Native Alaskans, while the other two-thirds were white settlers. Nome was a remote northern outpost locked in by ice for almost seven months of the year. The nearest railroad was 650 miles away, so the best means of communication was a US government-maintained mail track from Seward to Nome that was run by dogsled teams and their drivers, called mushers. The trail was almost one thousand miles across the treacherous Alaskan Interior, and typically took around a month to navigate.

So an impending epidemic was no joke, and would have ravaged a small, isolated town like Nome.

Diphtheria enters

Diphtheria is a highly contagious disease that attacks the throat and lungs. The Native Inuits in Alaska were particularly susceptible to it, and children were more likely to both be infected and die from it. When it struck Nome, the town's only doctor anticipated that, if it went unchecked, diphtheria would wipe out the entire town before help could arrive.

So Nome is nose-deep in both diphtheria and impenetrable ice when the call comes from Anchorage that they have the antitoxins that can stop the epidemic.

"Awesome," says Nome.

"But the planes can't fly in this terrible weather, you're totally icebound, and the nearest train station is seven hundred miles away from you," says Anchorage.

"Less awesome," says Nome.

"But," says Anchorage, "there may be another way . . ."

Since you read the title of this book, you've probably already guessed what that way was: dogs.

The earliest known use of dogsledding dates back to 1000 AD. It was developed by native Inuit people in northern Canada to transport food and supplies over the tundra. When white pioneers arrived at the Alaskan frontier, they found an established culture that relied heavily on the use of these sled dogs. The term *musher* to describe a dogsled team driver came from the French word *marche* (since the French were the first white people to plant their flag in Canada). *Marche*, meaning "walk" or "move," was used to command the team to start pulling. *Marche* became *mush* for English Canadians, and the term *musher* to describe the team driver arrived from there.

On the night of January 27, 1925, the first batch of 300,240 units of antidiphtheria serum were delivered by train to Nenana. They were wrapped in fur and weighed around twenty pounds. The antitoxins were immediately loaded onto the first of twenty sleds, pulled by more than one hundred dogs, who would relay the serum a total of 674 miles in life-threatening conditions to Nome. The temperature was sixty degrees below zero Fahrenheit. Mushers had to be sure not to run their dogs too hard or else the cold could frost their lungs and cause them to die of exposure, but time was of the essence. The entire route would ordinarily take twenty-five days, but in the brutal weather conditions, the serum would only last six.

I know, now it *really* feels like a movie. There's a ticking clock and everything.

Each leg of the run averaged thirty miles, with each of the twenty teams taking a leg, then handing off the antitoxins to the next team. Alaska's most famous musher, Leonhard Seppala, took on ninety-one miles alone, part of which was a dangerous shortcut over the Norton Sound. Seppala's lead dog, a Siberian husky named Togo, and his fellow dogs struggled for traction on the icy ground. Winds were strong enough that there was a risk the ice would break and send the team drifting out to sea. The temperature sank to eighty-five degrees below.

Miraculously, the team made it safely to the coastline only hours before the ice cracked.

Another famous musher, Gunnar Kaasen, set off on his leg of the run into a whiteout blizzard so strong that he couldn't see his own sled-dog team. His lead dog, Balto (who was disappointingly not part wolf nor voiced by Kevin Bacon, as I was led to believe by a 1995 animated movie), had to rely on scent to lead the team. When eighty-mile-per-hour winds flipped the sled and launched the antitoxins into a snowbank, Kaasen tore off his mitts and rummaged through the snow with his bare, frostbitten hands to retrieve it.

When Kaasen arrived in Port Safety, Alaska, on the morning of February 2 and discovered the next dogsled team wasn't ready to depart, he decided to take the serum the rest of the way himself. At five-thirty A.M., his team, led by Balto, barreled down the streets of Nome and delivered the serum to the doctor, saving the lives of the town residents and stopping a potential epidemic.

The relay took five and a half days. Of the 150 dogs that participated, four died of exposure on the trail. The Nome Serum Run received publicity all over the world and helped boost the inoculation campaign in the United States. Cases of diphtheria in the US were dramatically reduced as a result. Might I recommend you shout "DOGS DIED so your KIDS don't HAVE TO" next time you're arguing with your anti-vaxxer neighbor.

Today, the Nome Serum Run is commemorated each year with the Iditarod, a dogsled race in Alaska that runs one thousand miles between Anchorage and Nome. While the Iditarod path is actually based on the historic All-Alaska Sweepstakes race, it has many traditions that commemorate serum run to Nome along the way.

And even though it is a hellish trek through some of the most brutal country and conditions the world has to offer, for some reason, I really, really, really want to do it.

Probably because there are dogs.

---

sidebark

Huskies were introduced to North American from Siberia by a fur trader named William Goosak during the early twentieth-century Yukon Gold Rush to replace the Alaskan malamute, a larger and stockier sled dog. Huskies are smaller than malamutes, so they can pull faster, but still big enough to haul freight. Because of their size, Siberian huskies generate less heat, so they maintain their body temperature more effectively than malamutes. They also have a loping gait, meaning that one paw is always touching the ground, rather than a bounding gait like a greyhound. Bounders are ineffective at pulling sleds because the sleds pull them back every time they take flight. Huskies also have lots of very fine, highly twisted secondary hairs that form a special layer of their coat that traps warm air against the body, like a down jacket. Huskies can also use their large, fuzzy tails to ensure that they breathe warm air while they sleep. Each dog curls into a ball and covers its nose with its tail, which acts as a warm air filter.

When the Nome Serum Race is commemorated with a statue of Balto in New York's Central Park, there was much contention among the mushers who were involved in the run about whether it was fair for Balto to be memorialized, since he was one of many dogs involved, and since Togo was the lead dog on the longest leg of the run. It is this author's professional opinion that WHO THE FORK CARES? THEY WERE ALL GOOD DOGS.

Because people love to make things terrible, many of the dogs who ran the Nome Serum Run became side show acts. Balto and his team almost died from neglect in a Los Angeles carnival, but they were rescued by George Kimble, a businessman from Cleveland in 1927, and given a hero's welcome and a triumphant parade. The dogs were then taken to the Brookside Zoo, where they were well cared for for the rest of their lives. After he died, Balto's body was taxidermized and is still on display in the Cleveland Museum of Natural History.

HER MAJESTY'S CORGIS

How These Furry Potatoes Became the Symbol
of the British Crown

CORGIS · ENGLAND · 20TH CENTURY

When Thelma Evans was nine years old, her dog was run over by a car. The driver felt so horrible about the accident that he wrote to Thelma's parents, offering to give the family a new dog. Her parents declined, but when Thelma found out, she went rogue and wrote a letter of her own to the driver, saying she'd be happy to accept a new dog. But the driver didn't feel he could give her one without the permission of her parents.

The Twist?

The driver of that car was the future King George VI, and Thelma became one of the founding breeders of the line of royal corgis.

Funny little world, isn't it?

Corgis date back to the Vikings and were working dogs for hundreds of years in Wales. They herded sheep and cattle by nipping at their heels. The name *corgi* comes from combining two Welsh words—*cor*, which means "dwarf," and *ci*, which means "dog." The Kennel Club recognizes two kinds of corgis—Pembroke Welsh (the kind that the queen has) and Cardigan Welsh (which tend to be larger, longer, and darker).

In the late 1920s, Thelma bought her first two corgis off a farmer. She loved them so much that she cofounded the Welsh Corgi League for the purpose of their promotion.

Her stud dog, Red Dragon, became so famous that his puppies sold to English nobility, among them the Viscount of Weymouth. The viscount's kids then invited their friends Princesses Elizabeth and Margaret over to play with their dogs, and the princesses loved them so much that their father, the Duke of York, aka Albert Frederick Arthur George, aka the future King George VI, aka the accidental murderer of Thelma's childhood dog, decided to get them one of their own from the same breeder. Which was Thelma.

In 1933, Thelma (who did not tell the duke that she was the little girl whose dog he'd run over) brought the royal family their first corgi puppy, who they named Dookie. Dookie was so loved by the princesses that they soon acquired a second named Jane.

In the summer of 1936, when Elizabeth was ten and Margaret was six, a book of photographs called *Our Princesses and Their Dogs* was published. It just so happened to hit bookstores a few days before King Edward VIII abdicated the throne so he could cruise the Mediterranean with the American divorcée Wallis Simpson. The book was not only an adorable Christmas present for British youngsters, but also a

brilliant propaganda machine that assured the British public that the new king, George VI, was a decent family man living a very normal life with his very normal family and their adorable corgi puppies, unlike his profligate brother. The appearance of the corgis with the royal family also introduced the breed to England as an option for a pet, rather than just a farm dog.

IN AUGUST 1981, WHEN THE QUEEN'S FLIGHT LANDED IN ABERDEEN FOR HER ANNUAL BALMORAL HOLIDAY, IT WAS REPORTED THAT THIRTEEN CORGIS WERE WITH HER.

Years later, Elizabeth was given another puppy for her eighteenth birthday. She was registered under the name Hickathrift Pippa, which somehow turned into Sue, which evolved into Susan, proving that even the queen does the ridiculous thing where she comes up with nonsensical nicknames for her dogs that seemingly have nothing to do with their actual names. Whatever she was called, Elizabeth and Susan became inseparable. In 1947, hidden under blankets in the royal carriage, Susan rode with Elizabeth as she left with her new husband, Philip Mountbatten, for their honeymoon in Hampshire.

A year after Elizabeth and Charles's first child was born, Susan became a mother too. After going into heat, she was turned over to Thelma to be mated. Susan produced a pair of puppies—Sugar (who belonged to the infant Prince Charles) and Honey (who, in later years, lived with the Queen Mum)—from which all of the fourteen generations of royal corgis since have descended. This makes Susan the foundational bitch of the royal corgi lineage. Also, if I ever join a roller derby team, please let my name be The Foundational Bitch.

Since the 1950s, the queen has personally overseen a program of corgi breeding based on the grounds of Windsor Castle with the help of women like Thelma Evans. Post-World War II, the breed standards began to change to make them more pets than farm dogs. Now that they were no longer herding cattle, Corgis were bred to have longer, rounder bodies that hang lower to the ground. Their faces also got more adorably cartoonish. The queen has personally owned thirty corgis. In August 1981, when the queen's flight landed in Aberdeen for her annual Balmoral holiday, it was reported that thirteen corgis were with her. The queen has never allowed her corgis to compete in dog shows, or sold one, though she has given many as gifts.

Life as a royal corgi was pretty sweet. The queen's dogs had special quarters in the palace, which were known as the Corgi Room, aka my personal Good Place. They slept in raised wicker beds (to avoid drafts) and had fresh sheets daily. Each of the dogs received its own personal, individually designed menu, served to them by hand—sometimes by the queen herself. The dogs were fed in order of seniority on silver platters, and their menu included rotating dishes of steak, poached chicken, liver, and rabbit, along with homeopathic remedies and herbs for health. The queen walked them each day, and they traveled in chauffeured cars and private planes with the royal family.

If reincarnation exists, let me come back as a royal corgi.

Reports of their behavior vary. When filming their segment for the Olympic opening ceremonies in 2012, director Danny Boyle said the corgis did their part in one perfect take. But, like any young royals, they've had their share of headline-grabbing scandals. Members of the royal staff have claimed they're barely house-trained and prone to nipping at ankles. Princess Diana called them the royal carpet because they were always underfoot, and once became so tangled around the legs of the queen's personal footman that he tripped and was knocked unconscious. In 1954, our foundational bitch, Susan, bit the royal clock winder. A dog psychologist was called after the queen herself was bitten while trying to break up a fight among her pack—a fight that, perhaps not coincidentally, coincided with the breakup of Prince Charles and Princess Diana's marriage.

Around 2015, the queen stopped breeding corgis, stating that she didn't want to leave any behind when she died. In 2018, the last royal corgi died, bringing another great British dynasty to an end.

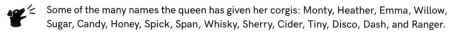

sidebark

🐾 Though the queen is most famous for her corgis, she also keeps "dorgis," which are dachshund and corgi crossbreeds. At the time of publication, the queen still has two dorgis, Candy and Vulcan (one can only hope the queen is a closet Trekkie).

🐾 Some of the many names the queen has given her corgis: Monty, Heather, Emma, Willow, Sugar, Candy, Honey, Spick, Span, Whisky, Sherry, Cider, Tiny, Disco, Dash, and Ranger.

🐾 Every Christmas, the queen personally makes stockings for each dog and fills them with toys and treats.

🐾 During their televised engagement, Prince Harry said the corgis never liked him but they adored Meghan Markle from the start. "I've spent the last thirty-three years being barked at," he said. "This one [Meghan] walks in, absolutely nothing. . . . just wagging tails, and I was like, 'Argh.'"

AMERICA'S FIRST SEEING-EYE DOG

The Walk That Changed History

GERMAN SHEPHERD · UNITED STATES · 1927

Morris Frank's life changed forever when he read an article in the *Saturday Evening Post*.

Technically, the article was read *to* him, because Morris was blind. He lost his sight in one eye after hitting a low-hanging tree branch as a child, then the other in a boxing match at age sixteen.

On November 5, 1927, the *Saturday Evening Post* ran an article titled "The Seeing Eye." It was written by an American woman named Dorothy Eustis. Dorothy and her husband were living in Switzerland, breeding and training German shepherds to be police dogs. However, Dorothy had had another idea. She had seen firsthand a school in Germany where dogs were being trained as companions for veterans who had gone blind from mustard gas in World War I. Her article talked about the program and the potential for dogs as companions and guides for the blind.

Morris was one of thousands of people who wrote to Dorothy after the article ran, but for some reason, his letter stood out. He wanted to know where he could get his own seeing-eye dog. "I want one of those dogs!" he wrote. "And I am not alone. Thousands of blind like me abhor being dependent on others. Help me and I will help them. Train me

and I will bring back my dog and show people here how a blind man can be absolutely on his own. We can then set up an instruction center in this country to give all those here who want it a chance at a new life."

Dorothy liked this idea. She invited Morris to her breeding kennel in Switzerland, Fortunate Fields, and introduced him to Kiss, a female German shepherd he renamed Buddy, who would become his companion. The deal was that Dorothy would give Buddy to Morris, but when Morris went back to America, he was going to become a publicity machine for the cause of the seeing-eye dog—a cause he happily took up for the welfare of other blind people like him. After six weeks of intense training together, Buddy and Morris returned to America, where they were met in New York City by floods of reporters. They all wanted to see what this dog was actually capable of. When one of the reporters asked if Buddy could lead Morris across the famously dangerous Wall Street, Morris said, "Just point me in the right direction."

He later wrote of crossing Wall Street that first day in New York, "[Buddy] moved forward into the ear-splitting clangor, stopped, backed up, and started again. I lost all sense of direction and surrendered myself entirely to the dog. I shall never forget the next three minutes: [ten]-ton trucks rocketing past, cabs blowing their horns in our ears, drivers shouting at us. When we finally got to the other side and I realized what a really magnificent job she had done, I leaned over and gave Buddy a great big hug and told her what a good, good girl she was."

He later telegrammed Dorothy a single word—SUCCESS.

With the story of Buddy making headlines across America, Morris and Dorothy opened a school called The Seeing Eye, named for Dorothy's article that brought them together. When it opened on January 29, 1929, it became the first guide dog training school in the United States.

Morris traveled through the United States and Canada, spreading the word about the Seeing Eye, guide dogs, and the need for equal-access laws for people who depended on those dogs. When he first brought her to America, Morris was routinely told that Buddy could not ride in the passenger compartment on trains with him. Thanks to his work, along with many other disability advocates, by 1935, all railroads in the United States had adopted policies specifically allowing guide dogs to remain with their owners on trains. In 1938, Frank and Buddy flew from Chicago to Newark, marking the first cabin flight by a seeing-eye dog and the passage of the United Air Lines guideline granting seeing-eye dogs the right to ride in plane cabins with their handlers. By 1956, every state in the country had passed laws guaranteeing blind people with guide dogs access to public spaces.

Today there are hundreds of organizations around the world that train dogs to be helpers and companions to the blind, in addition to people with a variety of disabilities. And while equal rights and accessibility for the disabled still has a long way to go, Morris and Buddy took it a big step forward with that historic walk.

sidebark

The same year Dorothy's article was published, United States senator Thomas D. Schall of Minnesota, who was also blind, was paired with a service dog imported from Germany. So Buddy wasn't technically the first service animal in America. However, the publicity and advocacy Morris and Buddy undertook was what really made the moment a movement and drew widespread attention to acceptance for service animals.

Some etiquette from the Guide Dog Foundation, for when you see a working guide dog or other service dog

* Don't touch, talk to, feed, or distract the dog while they are wearing their harness or vest. I KNOW. I also want to pet all the dogs always, but the handler's safety and mobility relies on the dog. Don't jeopardize that.
* Speak to the handler, not the dog.
* Do not give the dog commands; let the handler do that.
* Never grab or steer the person while their dog is guiding them or attempt to hold the dog's harness. You should ask if the handler needs your assistance.
* Always ask the handler where they'd prefer you walk.

RESERVOIR DOG

The Hoover Dam's Four-Legged Mascot

LAB · UNITED STATES · 1932–1941

Let's get something out of the way: The past was super racist.

The present is also super racist, but that's another conversation for another book.

Because the past was super racist, the dog we are about to discuss was given a name that is a racial slur. And I don't like that. But it wasn't this puppy's fault. He was still a good boy, and probably loved everyone because dogs don't see color. Literally.

So because this dog is good, but the men who named him had internalized the institutional racism of turn-of-the-century America, which manifested in their naming him, I'm not going to call him by his name. Since he was the Hoover Dam dog, we're going to call him Hoover.

As Americans began to colonize the western United States, they were faced with the daunting but essential task of harnessing the elements, including the Colorado River. The Colorado River, much like Miley Cyrus, couldn't be tamed. Every spring, it would rise to high, powerful levels that would break its flood banks and destroy homes and farms. When the water receded, the region was plagued with drought. The Colorado had to be regulated. But no one knew how to do that.

The government aspirationally approved Project: Tame the Mighty Colorado River—specifically, President Hoover approved it (get it? Hoover Dam?)—and in 1931, six construction companies joined forces to undertake one of the most ambitious building projects in US history. When completed, the Hoover Dam would not only control the Colorado, but would also supply electrical power and water to Las Vegas and the surrounding areas.

The first step of the process was diverting the Colorado River so that it would stay out of the way of the building site. Then the canyon had to be smoothed before concrete, which was poured into rectangular molds to harden and prevent cracking, was laid. With the Great Depression in full swing, there was no shortage of an eager workforce for the construction crew. In order to house all the workers and their families, a city was built near the project site, called Boulder City.

It was there, in a crawl space beneath the police station, where a tiny black Labrador puppy was first found. We don't know what happened to his mother or the rest of his littermates, but the dog became adopted by the whole town and soon had free rein of Boulder City.

And remember, we're calling him Hoover.

From puppyhood, men in the town began taking Hoover the dog with them to the construction site, and he became the unofficial mascot of the dam. Hoover joined the workers on the trip to the dam in the mornings and would ride back with them at the end of the workday. He might have also been part mountain goat, because he was able to navigate the impossibly rough construction site with ease. He would climb ladders, walk the catwalks, follow the men into the tunnels, and hop on the wooden platforms that lowered the men and equipment down into the canyon.

Every morning, Hoover would arrive at the project on the truck that brought workers from Boulder City to the dam. When the end-of-day whistle blew, he would line up with the men to leave. He was once seen cruising shotgun in the fancy car belonging to the chief engineer of the site, while the man's wife rode in the back seat. To get around the construction site, Hoover would ride the skips—small wooden platforms suspended from cables that would deliver the men and equipment down into the canyon. When he wanted to board a skip, Hoover would bark, and the operators would stop for him. He'd then bark again at the level of the dam where he wanted to disembark, no pun intended.

The town loved Hoover—too much, it seems, because the workers all wanted to share their lunches with him, and when he returned the town at night, everyone would feed him ice cream and candy. Eventually, he ate so many sweets he got sick. An announcement was placed in the local newspaper that read, "I love Candy but it makes me sick. It is also bad for my coat.

HOOVER JOINED THE WORKERS ON THE TRIP TO THE DAM IN THE MORNINGS AND WOULD RIDE BACK WITH THEM AT THE END OF THE WORKDAY. HE MIGHT HAVE ALSO BEEN PART MOUNTAIN GOAT, BECAUSE HE WAS ABLE TO NAVIGATE THE IMPOSSIBLY ROUGH CONSTRUCTION SITE WITH EASE. HE WOULD CLIMB LADDERS, WALK THE CATWALKS, FOLLOW THE MEN INTO THE TUNNELS, AND HOP ON THE WOODEN PLATFORMS THAT LOWERED THE MEN AND EQUIPMENT DOWN INTO THE CANYON.

Please don't feed me any more. Your friend, [Hoover]." After that, the commissary that prepared the workers' meals each day began to make healthy snacks for Hoover too, and soon they were packing him a lunch every day. He was even given his own lunch box, which he would carry in his mouth to the site. He would place the container alongside the worker's lunch pails at the dam site, and would eat with them when the lunch whistle blew. Hoover was so loved that, when one worker kicked him in anger, the rest of the crew jumped on the man and began to pummel him. Their vigilante justice was quickly put to a stop, but the kicker was escorted off the construction site and never came back.

When the Hoover Dam was completed in 1936, it was—and remains—a major engineering achievement. It still stands 726 feet high and has a crest width of 1,244 feet. The reservoir formed by the dam, Lake Mead, is one of the world's largest artificially created bodies of water. With the Colorado River under control, farmers received a dependable supply of water for the first time ever. Numerous cities such as Los Angeles, San Diego, and Phoenix were given an inexpensive source of electricity, which helped with population growth and industrial development. The dam's hydro-electric generators still provide electricity to Arizona, Southern California, and Nevada. The Hoover Dam also provided for flood control and irrigation.

In 1941, Hoover died in an accident on the construction site. The crew was devastated. One newspaper reported, "Rough, tough rock-hard men wept openly and unashamed." He was buried in a concrete slab on the site, and memorialized with a plaque. Because of his less-than–politically correct name, the plaque was replaced sans moniker, but still listing the many ways in which he was a very good boy.

sidebark

 The Hoover Dam was the site of the invention of the hard hat. Workers used to dip their hats in tar and let them harden in order to protect themselves from falling debris.

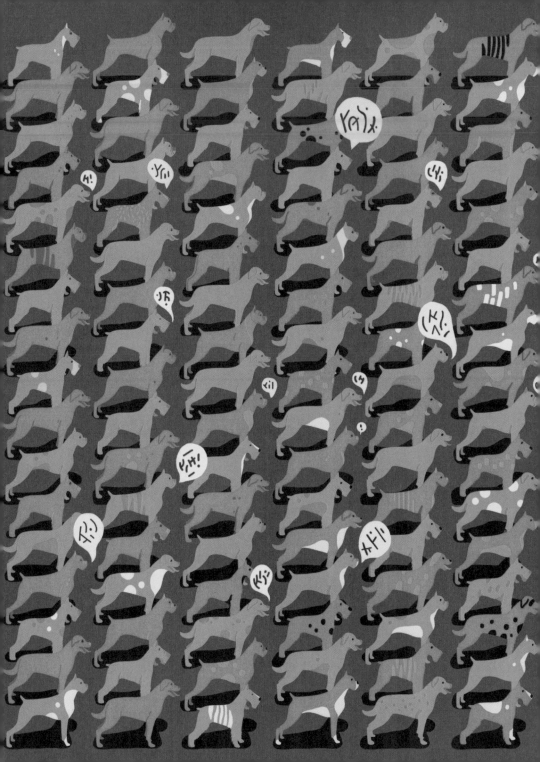

HITLER'S TALKING DOG ARMY

It Did Not Pan Out

AIREDALE TERRIER · GERMANY · 1940s

Of all the weird hot nonsense floating around pre–World War II Germany, there was a particularly odd craze for talking dogs.

Germany's first talking dog was Rolf, not named for the singing Nazi in *The Sound of Music* but definitely not an irrelevant correlation. According to his owner, Paula Morkel, Rolf could communicate by tapping out letters with his paw. Which, okay, maybe not outside the realm of possibility. But she then went on to claim Rolf was a poet and a bibliophile, spoke several languages, and dabbled in theology and philosophy. All via his tapping toes. And I get it, we all think our dogs are the smartest dogs ever and of course we are all right. But chill the fork out, Paula, jeez.

While Rolf was busy philosophizing and composing sonnets to the Third Reich, another dog was chatting up the citizens of Deutschland—Don, a German pointer, supposedly had the ability to say German words. No paw tapping for this pup—he made actual sounds. A journalist claimed that, when he asked the dog his name, the dog barked, "Don," in response. When asked "What do you have?" Don replied, "Hunger," and then demanded "cakes."

As a result of his chattiness, Don became an international celebrity and appeared in music halls and variety theaters across the world.

Rolf and Don both attracted attention in Germany because they rose to fame at the same time the New Animal Psychology movement was gaining followers. Led by Dr. Karl Krall, students of the movement believed that certain animals, such as dogs and horses, were nearly as intelligent as humans and, if trained correctly, had huge intellectual potential to unlock.

Know who was a big, big fan of this theory? The Nazis.

Hitler was a well-known dog lover—in spite of topping the list of "humans least deserving of the unconditional love of a dog," he had two German shepherds, Blondi and Bella. Hitler not only subscribed to this school of New Animal Psychology, but he also believed that police dogs could be trained to communicate with their SS masters and become soldiers for tasks such as guarding, reconnaissance, and surveillance. Not in the way that we've see dogs in war before—he thought these dogs could literally talk to their masters and serve in positions basically equal to those of human soldiers. While brutal guard dogs were used by the Nazis in concentration camps, the eventual goal was that the dogs would someday be the *only* guards needed at the concentration camps because of their training. Hitler sent Nazi officials to recruit intelligent dogs and

HITLER WAS TRYING TO CREATE AN ARMY OF TALKING, TELEPATHIC DOGS TO SERVE THE NAZIS.

enroll them in the Tier-Sprechschule ASRA, or Animal Speech School. There, they taught dogs the same methods Rolf and Don had used for communication, and even experimented in man-dog telepathy.

That's right: Hitler was trying to create an army of talking, telepathic dogs to serve the Nazis.

Seriously, who put this man in charge?

While the granddaughter of the school's headmistress denies that it was directly linked to the Nazis, historians have established clear ties between the school and Hitler's future goals for dog soldiers. And concern for animal welfare was a critical part of being a good Nazi. Part of the Nazi ideal was to be a friend to all animals, which is a nice sentiment until you remember that they were more concerned with animal welfare than with, you know, the millions of people they slaughtered.

There is no evidence that any of these experiments were successful, or that any of the training resulted in the SS walking around with talking dogs. The dogs never learned to heel Hitler.

YOU CALL THIS BARKAEOLOGY?!

Robot the Dog Discovers the Lascaux Cave Paintings

MUTT · FRANCE · 1940

The story goes that the Lascaux cave paintings were discovered by a teenager and his dog.

The story also goes that the Lascaux cave paintings were discovered by four teenagers and their dog.

The story also goes that the Lascaux cave paintings were discovered by five teenagers and their dog.

"The story goes" could be the tagline of history—it all depends on who's telling it.

There are two major players that all these stories have in common—Marcel Ravidat and his dog, a white mutt with a spot over one eye, named Robot. In 1940, Marcel, Robot, and possibly also his friends were hiking near Montignac, an area in the South of France that was still uninvaded by the Nazis.

Some accounts say that Marcel simply stumbled upon a weird hole in the ground and started exploring. There's also a version that says that Robot chased a rabbit, who disappeared down a hole, and Marcel went after him to investigate. In the stories where there are other teenagers involved, they may have been looking for rumored secret underground passages, which is why they had their eyes on the ground.

Whatever the case, I'm sure Robot was very helpful with the digging when they realized they had stumbled upon a vast network of underground caves covered in paintings that would change the understanding of prehistoric art.

Marvel and Robot had discovered the Lascaux caves.

The paintings found in the Lascaux caves are approximately fifteen thousand to seventeen thousand years old, making them some of the best-preserved and largest quantities of art from the Paleolithic period. The paintings in their halls depict mostly animals, including horses, deer, stags, cows, cats, and what some theorize are mythical creatures. Archaeologists believe that the caves were used over a long period of time as a center for hunting and religious rites. Whether the paintings represent the future hunting success their painters hoped for, or records of past hunts, we're not sure. What we do know is, during the Upper Paleolithic period, when these paintings were completed, Neanderthal man evolved into the version of Homo sapiens we all know and love today. At the same time, prehistoric art took a leap forward, as exemplified by the cave painting of Western Europe. Which is *best* exemplified in Lascaux.

The other thing that made the Lascaux caves unique was that the paintings were preserved so well, while most of what survived at other prehistoric art sites was just engravings. Although the area around Montignac is full of prehistoric murals, the paintings in the Lascaux caves are the only ones discovered where the original hues have not faded. A protective layer of chalk made Lascaux watertight, and by the time Marcel and Robot found them, they had been so completely sealed for so long that, even today, no one has found the actual entrance used by the prehistoric draftsmen who transformed their walls into a colorful menagerie. All we've got is that hole in the ground.

During World War II, the caves were used by the French Resistance to store weapons, but were opened to the public in 1948. They were closed again to prevent damage, and

THE PAINTINGS FOUND IN THE LASCAUX CAVES ARE APPROXIMATELY FIFTEEN THOUSAND TO SEVENTEEN THOUSAND YEARS OLD, MAKING THEM SOME OF THE BEST-PRESERVED AND LARGEST QUANTITIES OF ART FROM THE PALEOLITHIC PERIOD.

a replica is now open, should you ever find yourself in the middle of nowhere in southern France and looking for a way to spend an afternoon.

But, in spite of the role Robot played in finding the caves, dogs are not allowed.

One of the many great injustices of history.

THE DOGS OF WAR, PART II

The Pupper Privates of World War II

EUROPE · 1939–1945

There are, by my conservative estimate, ten bazillion stories of dogs in World War II. I could spend the rest of this book just talking about canine units in the war effort and what good boys they all were. So instead of making this a World War II-dogs book, I've chosen to focus on one battalion's pooch recruits that I found particularly incredible: D-Day's parachuting dogs.

In 1941, Britain put out a call for families to lend their dogs to the war effort. Which, for most dog owners, would be a hard pass. But remember—British families were struggling. Cities were being bombed and evacuated. Food was being rationed. One less mouth to feed and dog boarding until the war ended sounded pretty sweet. The dogs that were lent to the war effort were sent to the War Dogs Training School, which, I know, this is serious, war and all that, but if you are also imaging dogs doing drills in little uniforms, YOU ARE NOT ALONE.

Because so many people were hoping for somewhere safe to put their pets while they rode out the war, the school became more of a shelter (seven thousand dogs were sent in just two weeks), but many combat doggos did come out of it. Like any military academy and/or school for X-Men, dogs most fit for service were picked out of the masses and given special training for their mission. They were taught to be comfortable around loud noises. To sit still for hours on transport aircrafts. To identify the smell of explosives and detect mines. Trainers even went through battlefield scenarios with the dogs, such as what to do if their handler was captured, how to track down enemy soldiers, and how to behave during firefights.

Training for the Canine Corps lasted two months, but for certain dogs, it was only the beginning. The next phase of their study was parachuting.

I know, if you thought dogs doing military drills in smart little caps was adorable, parachuting dogs is TOO MUCH, but please, this is serious.

The dogs selected as paratroopers were about the same size and weight as bicycles, since parachutes were already being used to get bikes to British agents in occupied territories. The soldiers that worked with the dogs reported that they showed no fear jumping from the plane—and that they were lured to the ground with steak. They got dogs to jump out of planes in the same way I get mine to be in the same room as the vacuum cleaner—lots of treats. But the dogs apparently really liked jumping out of planes, and some would make the leap without any treats involved. Yet another thing dogs and I don't have in common.

The parachuting dogs were training for the D-Day invasion at the beaches of Normandy. When the 13th Parachute Battalion of the British army left for France, each of the three planes carried twenty men and one paradog—Bing, Monty, or Ranee, who were as ready for combat as the soldiers. They had trained for this in army.

On the ground, not all went smoothly for the paradogs. Monty was injured, and Ranee was separated from her troop and never seen again. But Bing, in spite of a rough landing that resulted in him getting caught in a tree, stayed with his battalion. Two more German shepherds were soon brought in to assist him. The three dogs led their paratroopers during their advance across Europe, sniffing out booby traps and land mines. Bing would freeze up and point with his nose when he sensed Germans, similar to a hound signaling its hunter its caught a game scent. They were also used to guard and patrol the camp.

After the war, Bing returned to civilian life, was renamed Brian, and lived out his days as a family dog. He was recognized with a Dickin Medal in 1947—an award for animal valor that is the equivalent of the Victoria Cross. He lived to the age of thirteen.

Bing and the paradogs were far from the only private pups in World War II, and I'd be remiss if I didn't mention a few more courageous canine combatants who loved treats and hated Hitler:

* World War II's most decorated dog was a collie–German shepherd–husky mix named Chips. Chips saw action in Germany, France, North Africa, and Sicily. Among his heroic exploits are his assault on an Italian machine-gun nest and helping take ten enemy Italian soldiers captive. Chips was awarded the Distinguished Service Cross, Purple Heart, and Silver Star for his actions; unfortunately, the commendations were revoked as military policy at the time didn't allow such recognition for animals. Boooooo.

* Rip was a stray dog adopted by the Air Raid Precautions in East London during the Second World War. During the Blitz, he helped locate people and animals buried in the debris after an air raid. Another dog, Jet, helped recover 150 people from debris after German air raids. When Jet located a woman buried in a bombed-out hotel in London, he refused to leave her side for twelve hours until rescuers reached her.

* Purebred English pointer Judy served as a mascot to the Royal Navy, and was captured along with her crew when their ship was torpedoed by the Japanese. Judy was taken to a POW camp, where she was adopted by Leading Aircraftman Frank Williams. Throughout their imprisonment, Williams kept her alive by sharing his rations. In return, Judy would bark and growl to distract guards when they beat POWs, and often left the camp to bring back food for the prisoners.

* Both the Allies and the Germans used dogs as messengers on the battlefields.

The speed record was set by German shepherd named Caesar, who delivered a message over 10.5 miles away in thirty-two minutes.

☙ Canadian and American dogsled teams were used to locate and rescue many downed pilots in Newfoundland, Greenland, Iceland, and Alaska. During the Battle of the Bulge, since transporting the wounded was difficult, hundreds of sled dogs were brought in with the idea they'd work as canine ambulances.

There are hundreds of stories of dogs involved in World War II. Some of these programs that employed these dogs were really racist and unsavory (not because of the dogs, obvi, but because of their racist, unsavory human counterparts). Some of them were heroic and amazing and used dogs in incredible ways. Some were, shall we say, morally ambiguous when it came to the treatment of animals. Some were not even ambiguous, they were just straight-out horrific—but this was a war.

As with all things, there is no single story of the dog in World War II.

---

sidebark

🐾 Ironically, the Allies' preferred breed of dog for fighting the Germans was the German shepherd. The dogs originated in Germany in the 1800s through selective crossbreeding of herding dogs (the first German shepherd was very Germanically named Horand von Grafrath), but after World War I, because of rampant anti-German sentiments, the dogs got a rebrand and became known as Alsatians in the UK. German shepherds were first introduced in the United States by soldiers returning home from World War I, but the breed didn't gain popularity until the canine film star Rin Tin Tin burst onto the silver screen (see "And the Pawscar Goes To . . .").

🐾 The most popular dog for combat in the Pacific Theater was the Doberman, also a German breed. They are named after a taxman, Louis Dobermann, who, after being met on his tax-collecting rounds with more than one hostile welcome, wanted to breed an imposing dog that would intimidate people into turning over their money quietly. They were originally called the Taxman's Dogs and are known for their loyalty and fearlessness. During World War II, the US Marine Corps Dobermans of the Pacific were known as the "Devil's Dogs," though their heroism was far more docile than the name implies (like all things with Dobermans, it's never as scary as it first appears). They delivered messages, ammunition, and medical supplies, and worked as sentries. Twenty-five of these dogs died in action at the Battle of Guam. Dobermans have earned an unfair reputation as vicious, because of their imposing compact frame and use in military and police action, but, like any dog, viciousness is not an inherited trait.

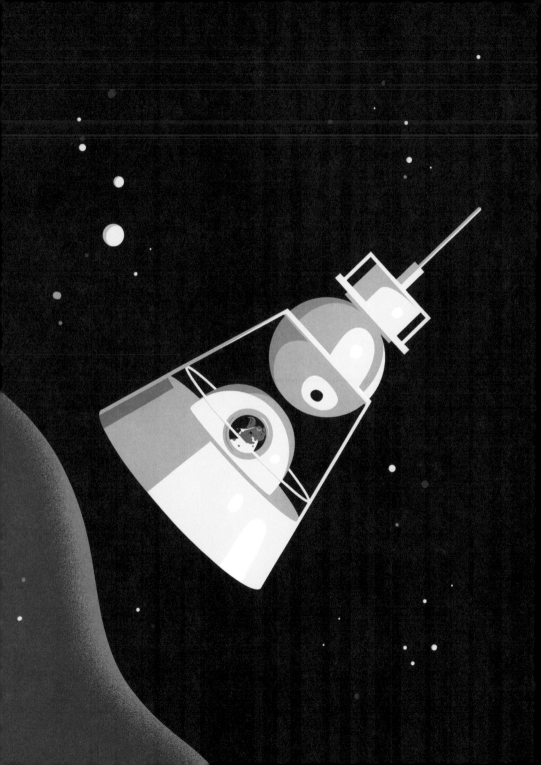

DOGS! IN! SPAAAAACE!

How Dogs Took Man to Space

TERRIER · RUSSIA · 1954–1957

To modern dog lovers, of which you are probably one, the practice of sending dogs into space alone and knowing they likely won't survive is super upsetting. And I'm not making excuses for using dogs as cannon fodder as humans tried to breach the final frontier. But the story of dogs in space is fascinating and an important part of the history of both man- and canine-kind.

In the early days of rocket science, no one knew what the effects of things like weightlessness, entering the atmosphere, and going into orbit would be on a mammal. Animals—mainly dogs, monkeys, and chimps—were used to test the safety and feasibility of launching a living being into space and bringing it back unharmed. Which—cool, cool, cool, not great, both because early space flight was essentially throwing tin cans into orbit and crossing your fingers, and also because, as previously discussed, JFC, let's stop experimenting on animals. But without animal testing, it would have been humans giving up their lives in man's quest to sail the stars. But also, how do you weigh the life of a human against an animal?

It's a complicated subject, yo.

Monkeys were the first mammals to make the jump into orbit, but the USSR switched to dogs because they were more trainable. They were also far more available—the streets of Moscow weren't crawling with stray orangutans, but there were puppies everywhere. Dogs' bodily systems are also not too different from humans', so the effects of space travel on them were good indicators of how the human body would react to zero gravity.

The first living creature to orbit the earth was Laika the dog, a terrier mix rescued from Moscow. Soviet scientists assumed that a stray dog would have already learned to endure harsh conditions of hunger and cold temperatures, so they were perfectly suited for survival in outer space. Which, yes, but also Russia and space are VERY DIFFERENT. American reporters dubbed the dog Muttnik, since she would be flying on board *Sputnik 2*. Laika and two other dogs were trained for space travel by being kept in small cages to help them get used to confined spaces and learning to eat a nutritious gel that would be their food in space.

In 1958, Laika was chosen from these three as the first dog to blast off. Unfortunately, her trip was never meant to be anything but one-way. She was only in orbit for a few hours before the craft overheated, and *Sputnik 2* burned up in the atmosphere. In a memoir written decades later after previously secret information had been released, a scientist who worked on *Sputnik 2* wrote that, before the launch, he took Laika home to play with his kids because he wanted to do something nice for her before she died.

My heart, but also, again, let's stop experimenting on animals!

THERE'S NO DENYING THE VALUABLE ROLE ANIMALS HAVE PLAYED IN HELPING ADVANCE SCIENCE, BUT THE LEGACY OF EXPERIMENTATION ON ANIMALS IS MESSY AND COMPLEX.

But the mission was a success. Laika had proved mammals could be in space! Now to figure out how to get them back alive . . .

The Soviet Union sent two more dogs, Belka and Strelka, into space on August 19, 1960, on board *Sputnik 5*. And good news— they survived, making them the first mammals successfully recovered from spaceflight. The Soviet Union used these dogs to study the effect of zero gravity on the brain, behavior, cardiovascular system, body fluids, electrolyte balance, metabolism, tissue development, and mating (also known as doggy style in zero G). In 1966, two more dogs, Veterok and Ugolyok, orbited for a record-breaking twenty-two days. Humans didn't beat the record until 1974.

During the 1950s and 1960s, almost thirty dogs were sent into space. Many of them did not survive the journey. But are they victims or heroes? Necessary sacrifices in man's quest to conquer the galaxy or unwilling participants in man's perilous ambition? Without dogs in space, progress in interstellar exploration could have cost a lot more human lives and taken much longer. There's no denying the valuable role animals have played in helping advance science, but the legacy of experimentation on animals is messy and complex. With modern regulations, animal testing is now under much closer scrutiny. While Russia continues to use monkeys in space tests, NASA has reduced the number of animal test subjects, and human astronauts now conduct the majority of experimentation.

But those dogs traveled to space. Laika boss.

MARTHA, MY DEAR!

Beatlemania's First Dog

OLD ENGLISH SHEEPDOG · ENGLAND · 1960s

So, who's your favorite Beatle? Is it John, the intellectual? Or maybe Paul, the romantic? George, the shy, mysterious one? Or is it Ringo, the goofball?

Personally, my favorite Beatle has got to be the loveable one. The mopsy-haired one with the affable personality who loved everyone. Perhaps not present in all the band's most memorable moments, but always loping along behind with her tongue hanging out and slobber dribbling from her jowls. The leader, if you will, of Sergeant Pupper's Lonely Hearts Club Band.

Fine, my favorite Beatle is a dog. Specifically, Paul McCartney's sheepdog, Martha.

Martha made the Fab Four five in 1966, at the height of Beatlemania. Paul had just moved into a new house in London with his girlfriend, Jane Asher, and decided he needed some canine companionship to complete their family. Soon, a floppy-eared sheepdog puppy joined them. Paul wanted to call her Knickers, but the breeder was so horrified when she found out that Paul agreed to change the dog's name to something much more traditional and far less cheeky—Martha.

The Beatles began in the 1950s in Liverpool, when teenagers John Lennon and Paul McCartney formed a songwriting partnership that would change the course of music history. After cycling through a few bassists and drummers, they added George Harrison, then Ringo Starr, and together they were the Beatles. After a residency in Hamburg, they returned to their native Liverpool, where they met and began working with manager Brian Epstein in 1962. He got the band shaped up, imposed rules like stop eating, swearing, and smoking onstage, and helped them develop a distinct, marketable image before shopping them around to record labels. In spite of rejections on the grounds that guitar groups were on the way out, Epstein eventually landed them a contract with UK label Parlophone Records. On June 6, 1962, they recorded in Abbey Road Studios, and soon after they had their first number one hit, "Please Please Me." From there, their rise was rapid and astronomical.

So why were the Beatles so popular, exactly?

Part of it was innovation. Part of it was timing.

Let's start with timing. The Beatles arrived on the scene in 1960s Liverpool and hit the United States in 1964 with their debut on *The Ed Sullivan Show*. In the early '60s, the first wave of post–World War II baby boomers were reaching their teens. And as youth are wont to do, they were looking to rebel against their parents' traditional values—a rebellion that was personified in the four mop-top Liverpudlians.

Not only did the postwar baby boom give the Beatles a much, much larger young audience than previous musical sensations, their irreverence personified everything the baby boomers wanted to be. Comments like John Lennon's saying the Beatles were bigger than Jesus made this brazen subculture into culture. The Beatles were also playing with gender norms—they covered songs by girl groups without changing the pronouns, sang in falsetto, and used a call-and-response style that wasn't typical of male singers—which mirrored the gender revolution of the '60s. Which, we know now, didn't really pan out, because people are still freaking the fork out over the singular *they*, but those youths can dream.

On to innovation. The Beatles introduced and popularized many concepts that define modern music, like comprehensive albums rather than single songs—prior to the Beatles, music was delivered mostly through 45s, which contained one or two singles and some filler. They also popularized the concept of large stadium concert tours. The first show of their 1965 North American tour sold out of all 55,600 tickets in seventeen minutes. It was the first concert held at a major outdoor stadium and set records for attendance and revenue. They weren't the first, but thanks to good old timing, they were the first to do it on a global scale. They were also one of the first popular bands that wrote their own music, and one of the first groups that functioned as a *group* rather than being fronted by an individual. They also popularized the music video, from the sawhorses and umbrellas of "Help!" to the piano-strung, upsettingly zoomed-in "Strawberry Fields Forever."

While Martha was never onstage or on-screen with the Beatles, she was a fixture backstage, and one of the gang—fortunately, as a sheepdog, she sported the mop-top haircut naturally. She brought out a different side of the Beatles, particularly Paul. He later said of her, "She was a dear pet of mine. I remember John being amazed to see me being so loving to an animal. He said, 'I've never seen you like that before.' I've since thought, you know, he wouldn't have. It's only when you're cuddling around with a dog that you're in that mode, and she was a very cuddly dog."

A few years after they adopted Martha, Paul and Jane Asher broke up. Not long after, the Beatles released the *White Album*, which included the song "Martha My Dear." Most people thought it was Paul mourning the break up with the great love of his life, but he later revealed the true meaning of the song: It was literally just about how great his dog was.

Martha lived to the ripe old age of fifteen and is still revered by many Beatles fans in the same way the Fab Four themselves are. One of Martha's offspring, Arrow, appeared on the cover of a Paul McCartney live album in 1993.

I CAN HAS RACIAL EQUALITY?

Nelson Mandela and His Dog, Gompo

RHODESIAN RIDGEBACK · SOUTH AFRICA · 1918–2013

It seems reasonable to expect that one of history's best, Nelson Mandela, was a dog person. Born in 1918 in South Africa, Mandela spent his entire political life involved in anticolonial and African nationalist politics. After the National Party of South Africa's white-only government established apartheid, he became one of the leaders of the movement dedicated to its overthrow.

Apartheid, an Afrikaans word meaning "segregation" or "separateness," was a system of institutionalized racial segregation that existed in South Africa from 1948 until the early 1990s. Apartheid was characterized by an authoritarian political culture based on *baasskap* (white supremacy), which encouraged state repression of South Africans of color for the benefit of the nation's minority white population.

Segregation was already alive and well in South Africa when the all-white National Party came to power—all they did was made it an official law. On paper it appeared to call for equal development and freedom of cultural expression, but in practice . . . not so much. Apartheid forced the different races to live separately, and grossly unequally. People had to register their race—the Population Registration Act of 1950 classified all South Africans as either Bantu (all black Africans), Coloured (mixed race), or white. Interracial marriages and any interracial social integration were banned. Black South Africans were forced to become citizens of a newly reestablished tribal organization rather than citizens of South Africa, thereby keeping them from serving in national politics. Behind all these laws was a ruthless political machine that brutally punished anyone who resisted.

It SUCKED. Apartheid SUCKED. It continues to suck—South Africa is far from a haven for racial equality today. Men like Nelson Mandela helped it suck slightly less.

Nelson Mandela served as president of the African National Congress, which was committed to overthrowing apartheid. Though his methods were initially nonviolent, he eventually founded an armed wing of the ANC, Umkhonto we Sizwe, which worked to sabotage the government. Because of this, he was arrested and jailed in 1962, and subsequently sentenced to life imprisonment for conspiring to overthrow the state.

But before all that, Nelson lived with

his family in Johannesberg, a family that included a Rhodesian ridgeback named Gompo. The Rhodesian ridgeback is distinguishable by a strip of hair down its spine that grows in the opposite direction of the rest of its coat. The breed is descended from the union of the now-extinct Cuban bloodhound and the hunting dog of the Khoikhoi people of South Africa. European colonizers used the dogs to harass lions and wear them out so they'd be easier to hunt.

The particularly cool thing about Nelson Mandela owning this Cuban dog is that Cuba's military assistance was a crucial factor in turning the tide against apartheid.

Many factors led to the demise of apartheid, but one of the most important was the defeat of the South African military in Angola by Cuba. In October 1975, South Africa invaded Angola with the intention of overthrowing the left-wing movement. And they would have gotten away with it too, except for the meddling thirty-six thousand Cuban soldiers that suddenly poured in to defend Angola. Fidel Castro sent these soldiers without really consulting any other world leaders, but it was effective in keeping the South Africans within their own borders. The Cuban victory in Angola over the South American government energized black Africa's fight against apartheid. In the words of Nelson Mandela, the Cuban victory "destroyed the myth of the invincibility of the white oppressor . . . [and] inspired the fighting masses of South Africa . . . [the defeat] was the turning point for the liberation of our continent—and of my people—from the scourge of apartheid."

After twenty-seven years, Nelson Man-

IT SEEMS REASONABLE TO EXPECT THAT ONE OF HISTORY'S BEST, NELSON MANDELA, WAS A DOG PERSON.

dela was released from prison. He went on to serve as president of South Africa. He was the country's first black head of state and the first elected in a fully representative democratic election. His government focused on dismantling the legacy of apartheid by tackling institutionalized racism and fostering racial reconciliation.

Segregation is far from over in South Africa. It's far from over in the world.

It's still a long walk to freedom. Better grab the leash and take a four-legged friend.

THE CANINE RESCUE TEAMS OF 9/11

Each One Gooder Than the Last

UNITED STATES · 2001

On September 11, 2001, the terrorist group al-Qaeda carried out a series of attacks against the United States. The three sites targeted by hijacked commercial airlines were the World Trade Center in New York City, the Pentagon in Washington, DC, and the White House, though the last was foiled by passengers on board the hijacked flights. The attacks killed 2,996 people (as well as thousands more who later died from diseases related to their proximity to the attacks), injured more than six thousand, and caused at least ten billion dollars in damage.

Within hours of the attacks on the World Trade Centers, nearly ten thousand volunteers converged on New York City to assist in rescue efforts and, later, cleanup. Around three hundred of those workers were dogs trained in search and rescue, therapy, cadaver recovery, police work, and bomb detection.

The first search-and-rescue dog on the scene in New York City was a German shepherd named Apollo, who worked with the K9 unit of the New York Police Department. He and his handler arrived fifteen minutes after the attack, and he was part of the initial group of dogs at Ground Zero trained to detect the scent of living humans in the rubble. Apollo looked for survivors eighteen hours a day for weeks after the attacks.

With the fires still raging at the site and the terrain unstable and unknown, dogs like Apollo navigated dangerous and unpredictable debris with their handlers to rescue survivors. Veterinarians were stationed at the site to help care for these dogs. Most dogs worked twelve-hour shifts, and they needed to have their paw pads, eyes, and noses cleaned frequently.

Workers came from all over the country to help with the aftermath, and the dogs came too. Thunder, a golden retriever trained to search for survivors of avalanches, accompanied his handler from Washington. He was one of many dogs at Ground Zero who had never been trained to deal with a disaster of that type or scale. The wilderness search-and-rescue (SAR) dogs in particular weren't accustomed to working in such noisy, filthy, difficult conditions, but many still rose to the task.

Just like humans, SAR dogs can become discouraged when they don't find anything, and handlers could sense the dogs'

disappointment when they found so few survivors at Ground Zero. Knowing the importance of keeping morale up, their handlers would hide and let the dogs find them so they could feel successful.

One of the most iconic images of 9/11 is a photo of a Riley, a golden retriever, in a basket being sent over a sixty-foot-deep canyon to search the rubble of the North Tower. Riley was trained to find live people in a disaster, and his handler later described their time together at Ground Zero: "Riley knew the people he continued to find were dead. He was never a formally trained cadaver dog. His job was to find the still living. I tried my best to tell Riley he was doing his job. He had no way to know that when firefighters and police officers came over to hug him, and for a split second you can see them crack a smile—that Riley was succeeding at doing an [altogether] different job. He provided comfort."

There were two dogs *inside* the World Trade Center when the planes hit: guide dogs, Salty and Roselle. Both dogs guided their owners out of the burning towers before they collapsed. Salty led his handler down from the seventy-first floor, and Roselle from the seventy-eighth, both descents taking nearly an hour. Michael Hingson, Roselle's handler, later said about that 1,463-step journey, "While everyone ran in panic, Roselle remained totally focused on her job. While debris fell around us, and even hit us, Roselle stayed calm." Hingson also remembered that, as they left the building, a firefighter entering stopped to hug Roselle.

Twenty-seven hours after the collapse of the Twin Towers, the last survivor was found by Trakr, a German shepherd who had made a fifteen-hour drive from Canada with his handler to assist with the rescue. When it became clear that the chances of finding survivors was slim, dogs trained to find cadavers and human remains were brought in in place of the search-and-rescue dogs. Later, these dogs were also used to find personal effects like jewelry, wallets, ID badges, and pieces of clothing that could be returned to victims' families.

Twenty-seven dogs also worked at the Pentagon to find survivors. Workers would excavate debris from the crash site and place it in a privacy area. The dogs would make a pass over the rubble and alert handlers to any scents. Workers would then go through the rubble with rakes to find the source of the dog's scent. One of those dogs was Sage, an eighteen-month-old FEMA search-and-rescue dog. The Pentagon was her first official mission, and she successfully located the body of the terrorist who had hijacked American Flight 77. The process was repeated for twelve days until all the debris had been sorted.

Today, all the dogs that worked on Ground Zero have crossed the rainbow bridge. The last surviving SAR dog—a golden retriever named Bretagne—died on June 6, 2016, just shy of seventeen years old, after working not only at Ground Zero but also with rescue missions after Hurricanes Katrina, Ivan, and Rita. In retirement, she served as a goodwill ambassador for a local fire department and a reading dog at local schools. Bretagne's handler, Denise Corliss, a volunteer firefighter with the Cy-Fair Fire Department, remembered a particular interaction during 9/11: "One man . . . started petting Bretagne and told me he didn't even like dogs. He knelt down beside her and told me that his best friend was missing. His friend really loved dogs and would be very upset if he didn't pet this dog."

When Bretagne was carried into the animal hospital to be euthanized, firefighters lined the sidewalks and saluted. She was carried out draped in an American flag.

Dogs have assisted in disaster relief and search-and-rescue efforts for hundreds of years on both large and small scales. Their assistance after the 9/11 attacks is certainly not the only example of heroism, but perhaps one of the largest-scale rescue efforts they were part of.

9/11 also opened new doors for therapy dogs. Dogs at Ground Zero and at Family Assistance Centers provided crucial relief for victims' families and first responders. Many people wouldn't speak to responders, but they would talk to the dogs. The four-legged therapists earned the name "comfort dogs" after a firefighter called the Veterinary Medical Assistance Teams and asked, "Where are those comfort dogs? They're the only thing that helps me get through the day." Therapy dog teams now provide support after all kinds of emergencies, from natural disasters to mass shootings.

File under: too good, too pure for this world.

sidebark

🐕 Only one dog—Sirius—died during the 9/11 attacks: He was in his kennel at the World Trade Center when the tower was hit and was unable to escape. Sirius worked with his handler, Port Authority Police sergeant David Lim, at the tower on a daily basis as a bomb-sniffing dog. Sergeant Lim was injured in the attacks but survived. Several months later, Sirius's remains were uncovered, and Sergeant Lim held a memorial in his honor.

🐕 Before Trakr, the German shepherd who found the last survivor of the wreckage, died, his DNA was entered into a cloning contest and was chosen for use. In June 2009, five Trakr clones were born.

FURGIN BIRTH

How Snuppy Became the World's First Cloned Dog

AFGHAN HOUND · SOUTH KOREA · 1996

In 2005, *Time* magazine declared that the Invention of the Year was . . . a puppy.

Before we all start petitioning for our dogs to be *Time*'s next cover model, let me explain—this particular puppy, an Afghan hound named Snuppy, was the first successfully cloned dog.

When Snuppy was first conceived—both literally and figuratively—many animals had already been successfully cloned. After Dolly the sheep was cloned in 1996, she had been followed by cloned cats, cows, horses, mice, mules, pigs, rabbits and rats. But no one had been able to clone a dog. Why?

Oh boy, I have to science. Hold on, let me focus.

Let's start with a breakdown of the most common type of reproductive cloning, which is called somatic cell nuclear transfer. It starts with extracting an egg from a female of the species, then removing the nucleus from that egg, which contains DNA. You do the same with a male's cell, then inject the nucleus from the male cell into the female egg. Electricity is then used to fuse the two eggs together, presumably applied by a man named Igor who dramatically throws an enormous third switch. The electricity mimics the union of sperm and egg and stimulates

cell division, thus forming an embryo. And if all this über-complicated science goes to plan, you implant that embryo into a female's uterus.

So why is this so hard to do with dogs?

Dogs don't experience regular ovulation cycles, and, while hormones can be used to jump-start ovulation in humans, canines don't respond to hormone treatments, so scientists are unable to predict or trigger it. When the bitch finally goes into heat, her eggs stay mature for just a few hours, which has left me imagining a team of scientists watching a dog twenty-four hours a day and then one of them pulling an alarm and screaming, "GO GO GO!" when it finally happens. If an egg is successfully extracted, a coating of fat makes it difficult to remove the nucleus.

So basically, everything. Everything makes it hard to clone a dog.

The first cloned dog was born April 24, 2005, after years of work by a team of researchers in South Korea. Led, disappointingly, not by Jango Fett, but by scientist Woo Suk Hwang, the goal of the project was to not only perfect the process of cloning but also study the health effects cloning has on animals, partly so that that research could someday be applied to humans. Some scientists were worried that cloned organisms were more prone to disease or that cloning sped up the aging process. Dolly the sheep died at just six years old—half the life expectancy of a sheep—and no one was sure whether that had to do with how she had come into the world.

Snuppy—a portmanteau of the initials of Seoul National University, where the experiment was completed, and the word *puppy*—was a statistical miracle even before he was conceived. Using a single cell from the ear of an Afghan hound, 123 surrogate mothers were used to carry 1,095 implanted embryos. Only three of these dogs got pregnant from those embryos. Of those three, one miscarried, and one other puppy was born successfully but died of pneumonia three weeks after birth. Snuppy was the only one who was not only carried to term by his yellow Lab mother but survived to adulthood.

When you do the math, the success rate of the project was less than two-tenths of a percent. In the words of Han Solo, "Never tell me the odds."

Snuppy lived his life as a lab dog, closely monitored and taken care of by the SNU team until he died from cancer at the age of ten. After his death, in a very *Inception*-y twist, the clone was then cloned. Scientists wanted to make sure Snuppy's terminal cancer wasn't a result of his cloning, so they implanted cells into three mothers, which bred four clone puppies born in 2017, one of which died a few days after it was born. The three surviving Snuppy clones were adopted by families and will live out their lives as pets, in order to monitor whether or not the environment a clone is raised in affects its life span and health.

It's too early to say what we'll learn from these cloned clones, but Snuppy's puppies will definitely be some of science's most important dogs. And, at just over a year old in 2019, they were reported to be very healthy and very fluffy.

sidebark

The Afghan hound's origins predate written history by a few thousand years. It's one of history's oldest purebred dogs—there's even a myth that Afghan hounds were the representative of the dog that Noah chose to take on his ark. Afghan hounds originated in the area that is now Afghanistan, India, and Pakistan as hunting companions and status symbols for royalty. The Afghan hound came to the West in the 1800s when European colonizers returned home with them, and quickly became a favorite breed of the British elite. They took a little longer to catch on in the United States, even though one of the first American owners was Zeppo Marx. The Afghan hound's popularity in the US finally soared when, in 1981, Barbie's new pet was unveiled: an Afghan hound named Beauty.

After Project Snuppy, lead scientist Hwang was caught up in a controversy that ultimately ended in his dismissal from the project and the university. He went on to use the technique he perfected at SNU to clone dogs for owners whose dogs had died. His next project? Cloning a woolly mammoth. A US company is also trying to do this, making it the next big scientific race. Begun, the Clone War has.

SLUM DOG MOUNTAINEER

From Homeless Stray to the First Dog to Climb Mt. Everest

MUTT · SOUTH AFRICA AND NEPAL · 2003

When Joanne Lefson visited northern India, she didn't expect to come home with the most adorable souvenir of all time: a stray puppy.

Joanne, a former professional golfer from South Africa, was already an animal activist and an avid traveler when she arrived in India. Years before, she had adopted her dog, Oscar, from death row at a South African shelter, and the two of them traveled to thirty-six countries together raising awareness for the plight of homeless dogs around the world.

When Oscar died in 2013, Joanne was adrift in the way we all are when we lose our dogs. She didn't know how to move on.

JOANNE AND RUPEE LEFT THE BASE CAMP DRAPED WITH A PAIR OF EMBROIDERED PRAYER FLAGS, WHICH THEY DEDICATED TO ALL THE HOMELESS DOGS IN THE WORLD.

Then, on her trip to India, she met Rupee.

Rupee was a homeless mutt living in a garbage dump. According to Joanne, when she found him, he was starving, dehydrated, and in such bad shape he could hardly stand up. But he managed to stumble over to her and collapse at her feet. He was eight months old. Joanne took him with her and nursed him back to health on a high-protein diet of rice and boiled eggs. Pretty soon, Rupee had returned from death's doorstep and was an energetic bundle of golden floof and floppy ears I want to scratch SO BAD.

Joanne already had a trek to Mount Everest base camp planned for later that year—but she had expected to be doing it with Oscar. It felt wrong to be going at it alone.

But there was Rupee, adorable and golden and fluffy and determined to survive anything.

She decided to take him with her instead.

After he was cleared for the trip by his vet, Rupee and Joanne traveled to Kathmandu, where they began their trek accompanied by several porters, guides, and a videographer. Along the way they faced snow delays, rainstorms, landslides, mud-slides, and a yak attack, all while traveling along wobbly bridges and treacherous, icy mountain paths. Joanne was concerned that the altitude would make Rupee sick, so she hired an extra porter to accompany them with a basket, in case Rupee couldn't walk. But because he was born in the Himalayas, the altitude didn't bother him a bit. He was also too delighted by the snow—his first time seeing it—to notice or be scared by the height. Joanne reported that, most days, Rupee ended up leading the group.

Jopee (will think of better celebrity couple name later) reached the Everest base camp on October 26, 2013. Important distinction: Rupee didn't make it to the *summit* of Everest, as several sensationalized headlines reported. He made it to the *base camp*. But that's no small feat for such small feet! It was a ten-day trek to reach the camp, which is located more than seventeen thousand feet above sea level. He also may not have been the first dog there. Several other climbers reported previously seeing strays take up residence at the base camp. But Rupee was the first dog officially on the record as making the trek.

Joanne and Rupee left the base camp draped with a pair of embroidered prayer flags, which they dedicated to all the homeless dogs in the world.

DYING BREEDS

Extinct Dog Breeds in History

Dogs are one of the most diverse species on the planet. If you think too hard about the fact that Chihuahuas and Great Danes come from the same genetic stock, your head will explode. And, like any widely varied species, certain types of dogs come and go. Here's a look at five breeds that don't exist anymore but left an important mark on our modern dogs.

Turnspit Dog

The turnspit was a part of nearly every kitchen in sixteenth-century Britain. Meat was roasted over open fires and had to be turned constantly so it would cook evenly. Since nobody got time for that, a wooden wheel was often mounted on the wall near the fireplace, which would then be attached to a chain connected to the spit. A dog was then placed in the wheel and would run to turn the spit.

It's a giant hamster wheel attached to the wall and with a dog running in it. That's the general idea.

Turnspit dogs were viewed as kitchen utensils, pieces of machinery rather than pets. They were small and short, with crooked front legs and droopy ears—basically an ugly corgi. The turnspit dogs were bred to be small but also strong and sturdy, since they had to work for long hours. Zoologist Carl Linnaeus named them *Canis vertigus*, which is Latin

for "dizzy dog," because they were turning all the time. Their tails were usually cut off so as not to get caught in the wheel. The turnspit dogs worked in the kitchens of large estates every day but Sunday—like they rest of the staff, they had that day off, and would sometimes go to church with the family.

Darwin cited the turnspit dogs as an example of genetic engineering and evolution for a task. "Look at the spit dog," he said. "That's an example of how people can breed animals to suit particular needs." Even Shakespeare mentions them in *The Comedy of Errors*.

By 1850, the role of the turnspit dog had entirely flipped. Instead of a sign of wealth, a dog roasting your meat instead of owning a newfangled meat-turning machine called a clock jack was so last century. Since they were not particularly attractive and had never before been thought of as pets, the breed eventually went extinct. By 1900, the turnspit dogs were turning no more.

St. John's Water Dog

The St. John's water dog, also known as the lesser Newfoundland, was the ancestor of most modern retrievers and Labradors. They were brought to the Canadian island of Newfoundland by the Portuguese fishermen sometime in the sixteenth century. Newfoundland had been colonized at various

times in history but had been largely unin-habited for around two hundred years when European settlers arrived.

The St. John's water dogs were known for being excellent swimmers, and their short coats didn't drag them down when wet. The dogs were as at home in the water as they were on land and specialized in retrieving nets, lines, and ropes for their fishermen. Some even dove underwater to retrieve fish that had slipped from their hooks.

During the nineteenth and early twen-tieth centuries, St. John's water dogs were exported from Newfoundland to England, where they were crossbred with other dogs to create the retrievers and Labradors that became the hunting dogs of the aristoc-racy. However, in Newfoundland, the dogs began to die out. In a nineteenth-century attempt to encourage sheep raising, heavy taxes were placed on any dogs that weren't sheep-related.

St. John's water dogs resembled modern Labradors. They were all black except for white patches on their chest and paws and had dense, oily, waterproof coat and thick tails. Their ears were more forward-fac-ing than those of the floppy-eared Labs we know today.

When the breed was exported from Canada to England, it split into two. The larger ones went on the become the mod-ern-day Newfoundland, while the smaller ones became Labradors, which in turn spawned other breeds such as the flat-coated retriever, curly-coated retriever, Chesapeake Bay retriever, golden retriever, and Labrador retriever. Over time, the Lab-rador has become the world's most popular dog breed.

Salish Wool Dog

The Salish are an indigenous group in the Pacific Northwest of North America, known for their finely woven blankets. Before the Europeans arrived, the blankets were high in trade value and important in ceremonies such as marriages and funerals. However, the Salish people didn't have sheep, and therefore no wool to make these blankets out of.

Which means that many of these blan-kets were made from the fur of dogs. One particular kind of dog.

The Salish wool dog was kept for the production of wool from its thick, soft inner coat. They were described by Euro-pean explorer Captain George Vancouver as resembling, but somewhat larger than, a Pomeranian. The woolly dogs were sheared once a year, and the fur was mixed with dif-ferent materials for weaving blankets and other textiles.

Since the Salish people also used coyote-like short-haired dogs for hunting and protection, the woolly dogs were kept separate on their own small islands to pre-vent interbreeding. They were fed mainly salmon, which contributed to their thick, lustrous coats.

The Salish wool dog went extinct in the mid-nineteenth century due to the intro-duction of sheep and large-scale machin-ery brought by European settlers, yet again proving that white people ruin everything.

Hawaiian Poi Dog

Dogs were brought to Hawaii with the first Polynesian settlers between 300 and 800 CE. The poi dog got its name from poi, a common food made from fermented taro roots. Meat was expensive, so the dogs mostly subsisted on a diet of poi. Since there were no large mammals in Hawaii and the dogs weren't needed for herding or protection, they were primarily used as companions, particularly for children. A puppy was often given to an infant at birth, and the baby and the puppy would be breastfed together, which was believed to give the dog more protective instincts over the child.

Because of their mostly starch diet, the poi dogs suffered many health problems, but they were friendly and playful. They were small, didn't bark much, and tended to have large, distended potbellies because of their diet. Over generations of breeding, their heads became flat, because chewing poi does not require strong jaw muscles. The dogs were also sometimes eaten as a delicacy at religious feasts.

By the early twentieth century, the poi dog went extinct as Westerners began to invade the Polynesian islands and native religious ideas were abandoned. The Hawaiian poi dogs began to mix with dogs of European settlers and were gradually replaced by crossbreeds.

Old English Bulldog

The Old English bulldog was descended from ancient war dogs like the mastiff, and bred for the totally depraved and horrific sports of bull- and bearbaiting. The mastiff was too slow for the sport, so in the 1100s, it was crossed with the greyhound to create the Old English bulldog.

The breed's decline began in England with the passage of the Cruelty to Animals Act of 1835. Bullbaiting and dog fighting were outlawed (way overdue), which led to a lack of interest in perpetuating the Old English bulldog and other bully breeds, like bullenbeisser, which was the German equivalent.

Despite the laws making dog fighting illegal, the sport continued for many years. Breeders determined a cross between the Old English bulldog and Old English terrier created a super-fast and nimble fighting dog. This new breed of dog, called the bull and terrier, was a precursor to the modern bull terrier and American pit bull, and its emergence accelerated the extinction of the Old English bulldog.

Another factor in the extinction of the Old English bulldog was their becoming pets. Because people preferred companion dogs to be smaller, they started breeding the bulldog with pugs or terriers until the ideal size for a pet bulldog was eight pounds. These dogs became known as toy bulldogs and were popular with the working class who wanted dogs but lived in small quarters.

So what about those adorable, wrinkly, snorey, snarfly pups that I follow on Instagram? Aren't those Old English bulldogs? Kind of. They're technically Olde English Bulldogges, which were created by breeders in the 1970s in order to re-create the Old English bulldog, but the original breeding stock has died out.

SELECTED BIBLIOGRAPHY

General

Albee, Sarah. *Dog Days of History: The Incredible Story of Our Best Friends.* Washington, DC: National Geographic Kids, 2018.

American Kennel Club. http://www.akc.org.

Bondeson, Jan. *Amazing Dogs: A Cabinet of Canine Curiosities.* Ithaca, NY: Cornell University Press, 2011.

Coren, Stanley. *Gods, Ghosts, and Black Dogs: The Fascinating Folklore and Mythology of Dogs.* Dorset, UK: Hubble & Hattie, 2016.

————. *The Pawprints of History: Dogs and the Course of Human Events.* New York: Free Press, 2002.

Derr, Mark. *A Dog's History of America: How Our Best Friend Explored, Conquered, and Settled a Continent.* New York: North Point Press, 2004.

The Dog Encyclopedia: The Definitive Visual Guide. New York: DK Publishing, 2013.

Hobgood-Oster, Laura. *A Dog's History of the World: Canines and the Domestication of Humans.* Waco, TX: Baylor University Press, 2014.

Méry, Fernand. *The Life, History, and Magic of the Dog.* New York: Grosset & Dunlap, 1970.

Miklósi, Ádám. *The Dog: A Natural History.* Princeton, NJ: Princeton University Press, 2018.

White, Emma. *A History of Britain in 100 Dogs.* Stroud, UK: The History Press, 2017.

Dog Domestication

Chan, Melissa. "The Mysterious History Behind Humanity's Love of Dogs." *Time,* August 25, 2016. http://time.com/4459684/national-dog-day-history-domestic-dogs-wolves/.

Handwerk, Brian. "How Accurate Is *Alpha*'s Theory of Dog Domestication?" *Smithsonian.com,* August 15, 2018. https://www.smithsonianmag.com/science-nature/how-wolves-really-became-dogs-180970014/.

Lallensack, Rachael. "Ancient Genomes Heat Up Dog Domestication Debate." *Nature,* July 18, 2017. https://www.nature.com/news/ancient-genomes-heat-up-dog-domestication-debate-1.22320.

Yong, Ed. "A New Origin Story for Dogs: The First Domesticated Animals May Have Been Tamed Twice." https://www.theatlantic.com/science/archive/2016/06/the-origin-of-dogs/484976/.

Dogs in Ancient Egypt

Dunn, Jimmy. "The Dogs of Ancient Egypt." Tour Egypt, n.d. http://www.touregypt.net/featurestories/dogs.htm.

MacDonald, James. "For Pets in Ancient Egypt, Life Was Hard (or Really Easy)." JSTOR Daily, July 1, 2015. https://daily.jstor.org/pets-ancient-egypt-life-hard-really-easy/.

Mark, Joshua J. "Dogs in Ancient Egypt." *Ancient History Encyclopedia,* March 13, 2017. https://www.ancient.eu/article/1031/dogs-in-ancient-egypt/.

The Xoloitzcuintli

Becker, Dr. Karen. "Hairless Dogs, Revered Since Ancient Times, Enjoy Modern-Day Following." Healthy Pets. May 25, 2017. https://healthypets.mercola.com/sites/healthypets/archive/2017/05/25/hairless-dog-breeds.aspx

Romey, Kristin. "This Hairless Mexican Dog Has a Storied, Ancient Past." *National Geographic,* November 22, 2017. https://news.nationalgeographic.com/2017/11/hairless-dog-mexico-xolo-xoloitzcuintli-Aztec/.

"Xoloitzcuintli." DogTime, n.d. https://dogtime.com/dog-breeds/xoloitzcuintli.

Panhu

Dhwty, "A Loyal Companion and Much More: Dogs in Ancient China." Ancient Origins, November 27, 2015. https://www.ancient-origins.net/history-ancient-traditions/loyal-companion-and-much-more-dogs-ancient-china-004695.

Liu Jue. "'Tails' of Ancient Dogs." The World of Chinese, February 27, 2018. https://www.theworldofchinese.com/2018/02/tails-of-ancient-dogs/.

Argos, the Dog of the *Odyssey*

"Dogs for the Ancient Greeks." Kosmos Society, Center for Hellenic Studies, Harvard University, n.d. https://kosmossociety.chs.harvard.edu/?p=35627.

Higgins, Charlotte. "The *Iliad* and What It Can Still Tell Us About War." *The Guardian,* January 29, 2010. https://www.theguardian.com/books/2010/jan/30/iliad-war-charlotte-higgins.

Mitchell, Stephen. "The Death of Argos." *The New Yorker,* September 16, 2013. https://www.newyorker.com/magazine/2013/09/23/the-death-of-argos.

King Yudisthirn and the Dog of Indian Lore

Mahabharata, section XXIII. "The Story of Yudhisthira (Dharmaraja)." Mahabharata Online, n.d. http://www.sacred-texts.com/hin/m07/m07023.htm.

Mahabharata, section XCV. https://web.archive.org/web/20100116130453/http://www.sacred-texts.com/hin/m01/m01096.htm. https://www.mahabharataonline.com/stories/mahabharata_character.php?id=59.

Peritas

"Alexander the Great and the Situation . . . The Great? Crash Course World History #8." CrashCourse, March 15, 2012. https://www.youtube.com/watch?v=0LsrkWDCvxg.

Mark, Joshua J. "Alexander the Great." *Ancient History Encyclopedia*, November 14, 2013. https://www.ancient.eu/Alexander_the_Great/.

The Pekingese
"History of the Pekingese." Pekingese Central, n.d. https://pekingesecentral.com/history-of-the-pekingese/.

"Origin of Pekingese." The Pekingese Club of America, n.d. http://thepekingeseclubofamerica.net/docs/origin.pdf.

Dionne, Mary-Jo. "The Pekingese: From the Palace to the People: The History Behind a Little Prince of a Puppy." *Modern Dog*, n.d. https://moderndogmagazine.com/breeds/pekingese.

The Dog King of Norway
"The Dog Who Was King of Norway." Labrador Collectibles, April 29, 2017. https://www.labradorcollectibles.com/blogs/news/the-dog-who-was-king-of-norway.

Fritz, Robb. "History's a Bitch: A Dog Walk Through Time: This Dog Rules." *McSweeney's*, October 26, 2011. https://www.mcsweeneys.net/articles/this-dog-rules.

LeBlanc, Tyler. "The Dog Kings of Scandinavia." Modern Farmer, June 11, 2014. https://modernfarmer.com/2014/06/dog-kings-scandinavia/.

The Dog of St. Roch
Filz, Gretchen. "The Story of St. Roch, Patron Saint of Dogs and Dog Lovers." The Catholic Company, August 16, 2017. https://www.catholiccompany.com/getfed/st-roch-patron-of-dogs-6114.

"St. Rocco, Patron Saint of Dogs." Eco Hvar, Croatia, n.d. http://www.eco-hvar.com/en/highlights/81-st-rocco-patron-saint-of-dogs.

Robert the Bruce's Dog
Coile, Caroline. "Get to Know the Scottish Deerhound: Hound of the Moors." Dogster, November 23, 2015. https://www.dogster.com/lifestyle/get-to-know-the-scottish-deerhound-hound-of-the-moors.

Perritano, John. "10 Dogs Who Made History." HowStuffWorks.com, March 17, 2018. https://animals.howstuffworks.com/pets/10-dogs-who-made-history9.htm.

"The Dog Behind Braveheart—and the American Revolution!" DogKnowledge.net, n.d. http://dogknowledge.net/dog-stories-and-facts/dog-stories/the-dog-behind-braveheart-and-the-american-revolution.php.

Conquistadors' Dogs
"Becerrillo (The Soldier Dog That Put the Conquistadors to Shame)." EasyPetMD, n.d. https://www.easypetmd.com/becerrillo-soldier-dog-put-conquistadors-shame-sam-stall.

"Dogs of the Conquistadors." Weapons and Warfare, January 12, 2019. https://weaponsandwarfare.com/2019/01/12/dogs-of-the-conquistadors/.

Yuhas, Alan. "Conquistadors Sacrificed and Eaten by Aztec-Era People, Archaeologists Say." *The Guardian*, October 10, 2015. https://www.theguardian.com/world/2015/oct/10/conquistadors-sacrificed-eaten-aztec-acolhuas.

Pompey the Pug
"Brave Pug of William of Orange." Pup.com, n.d. https://www.pup.com/stories/brave-pug-of-william-of-orange/.

O'Connell, Rebecca. "12 Fun Facts About Pugs." Mental Floss, http://mentalfloss.com/article/64051/12-snuffly-facts-about-pugs.

Urian the Greyhound
History.com editors. "Henry VIII." History, A&E Television Networks, updated April 1, 2019. https://www.history.com/topics/british-history/henry-viii.

Jan (username). "How the History of England Was Changed by a Dog." *The Poodle (and Dog) Blog*, February 26, 2009. https://thepoodleanddogblog.typepad.com/the_poodle_and_dog_blog/2009/02/how-the-history-of-england-was-changed-by-a-dog.html.

Dogs of the English Civil War
"The Dogs of War: Prince Rupert and Sergeant Major General Boye." EsoterX, January 1, 2015. https://esoterx.com/2015/01/01/the-dogs-of-war-prince-rupert-and-sergeant-major-general-boye/.

Grundhauser, Eric. "375 Years Later, English Schoolchildren Still Learn About a Magic Propaganda Dog." Atlas Obscura, March 22, 2018. https://www.atlasobscura.com/articles/prince-rupert-magic-dog-called-boy.

"A Short History of Poodle Grooming." Pedigree.com, n.d. https://www.pedigree.com/dog-care/dog-facts/a-short-history-of-poodle-grooming#.

Diamond and Isaac Newton
Messenger, Stephen. "How Newton's Spunky Dog Nearly Robbed Us of the Laws of Gravity." The Dodo, July 7, 2015. https://www.thedodo.com/isaac-newtons-dog-gravity-1236801516.html

"When Sir Isaac Newton's Dog Caused a Fire." *Dog with Blog*, n.d. https://dogwithblog.in/diamond-newtons-dog/.

The Dog Shogun
"The Dog Shogun, Tokugawa Tsunayoshi." JapanWorld, July 18, 2015. https://japanworld.info/blog/the-dog-shogun-tokugawa-tsunayoshi/.

Wallin, Lisa. "The Story of the Japanese Shogun Who Believed He Was a Dog in a Previous Life." Tokyo Weekender, November 1, 2017. https://tokyoweekender.com/2017/11/the-story-of-the-japanese-shogun-who-believed-he-was-a-dog-in-a-previous-life/.

Barry the St. Bernard
Blumberg, Jess. "A Brief History of the St. Bernard Rescue Dog." *Smithsonian.com*, https://www.smithsonianmag.com/travel/a-brief-history-of-the-st-bernard-rescue-dog-13787665/.

"History of the Breed." Saint Bernard Club of America, n.d. https://saintbernardclub.org/history-and-breed-standard/history-of-the-breed/.

Kas, Dimitri. "The St Bernard: The Making of an Alpine Legend." House of Switzerland, updated April 26, 2019. https://www.houseofswitzerland.org/swissstories/history/st-bernard-making-alpine-legend.

"If You Want a Friend in Washington, Get a Dog"
Lee, Shaune. "A Dog's Life for Laddie Boy." *Boundary Stones* (blog), WETA, August 20, 2018. https://blogs.weta.org/boundarystones/2018/08/20/dog%E2%80%99s-life-laddie-boy.

Presidential Pet Museum. http://www.presidentialpetmuseum.com.

Tedeschi, Diane. "The White House's First Celebrity Dog." *Smithsonian Magazine*, January 22, 2009. https://www.smithsonianmag.com/history/the-white-houses-first-celebrity-dog-48373830/.

Fortune the Pug
Coren, Stanley. "The Dogs of Napoleon Bonaparte." *Psychology Today*, March 8, 2018. https://www.psychologytoday.com/us/blog/canine-corner/201803/the-dogs-napoleon-bonaparte.

Mather, Ruth. "The Impact of the Napoleonic Wars in Britain." British Library, May 15, 2014. https://www.bl.uk/romantics-and-victorians/articles/the-impact-of-the-napoleonic-wars-in-britain.

"The Canine Ups and Downs of Napoleon Bonaparte." National Purebred Dog Day. November 1, 2017. https://nationalpurebreddogday.com/the-canine-ups-and-downs-of-napoleon-bonaparte/.

Seaman, Lewis, and Clark
"Seaman." National Park Service, updated April 10, 2015. https://www.nps.gov/jeff/learn/historyculture/seaman.htm.

"Travel the Lewis and Clark Trail: Seaman—Lewis's Newfoundland Dog." LewisAndClarkTrail.com, n.d. http://lewisandclarktrail.com/seaman.htm.

"What happened to Seaman After the Lewis and Clark Expedition?" National Park Service, n.d. https://www.nps.gov/articles/what-happened-to-seaman-after-the-lewis-and-clark-expedition.htm.

Boatswain and Lord Byron
Bond, Geoffrey. "Byron and His Dogs—in Pictures." *The Guardian*, December 3, 2013. https://www.theguardian.com/books/gallery/2013/dec/03/byron-dogs-pictures.

Taylor, Michelle M. "The Curious Case of 'Epitaph to a Dog': Byron and *The Scourge*." *The Byron Journal* 43, no. 1 (2015). https://online.liverpooluniversitypress.co.uk/doi/abs/10.3828/bj.2015.6?journalCode=bj&.

Whitfield, David. "This Collar from Byron's Dog Shows Its Battle Scars—from Fighting with the Poet's Bear." *NottinghamshireLive*, November 3, 2017. https://www.nottinghampost.com/news/news-opinion/collar-byrons-dog-shows-battle-715429.

Pavlov's Dogs and the Brown Dog Affair
Doshi, Neel, and Lindsay McGregor. "The Fallacy of Pavlov's Dog." *Psychology Today*, November 5, 2015. https://www.psychologytoday.com/au/blog/primed-perform/201511/the-fallacy-pavlovs-dog.

"The Physiologists vs. the Antivivisectionists: The Brown Dog Affair." The Psychological Society, n.d. http://www.physoc.org/sites/default/files/page/Info_Sheet_Brown_Dog_Affair.pdf.

Specter, Michael. "Drool: Ivan Pavlov's Real Quest." *The New Yorker*, November 17, 2014. https://www.newyorker.com/magazine/2014/11/24/drool.

White, Emma. "The Brown Dog Affair." From *A History of Britain in 100 Dogs*. https://www.thehistorypress.co.uk/articles/the-brown-dog-affair/.

Greyfriars Bobby
Alleyne, Richard. "The Legend of Greyfriars Bobby Really Is a Myth." *The Telegraph*, August 3, 2011. https://www.telegraph.co.uk/news/uknews/8679341/The-legend-of-Greyfriars-Bobby-really-is-a-myth.html.

"Greyfriars Bobby: The Most Loyal of Little Dogs, or a Victorian Era Publicity Stunt?" Atlas Obscura, n.d. https://www.atlasobscura.com/places/greyfriars-bobby.

Johnson, Ben. "Greyfriars Bobby." Historic UK, n.d. https://www.historic-uk.com/HistoryUK/HistoryofScotland/Greyfriars-Bobby/.

Fido
"Abraham Lincoln's Fido." Presidential Pet Museum, n.d. http://www.presidentialpetmuseum.com/abraham-lincolns-fido/.

Coren, Stanley. "Why Are Dogs So Frequently Called 'Fido'?" *Psychology Today*, October 12, 2011. https://www.psychologytoday.com/au/blog/canine-corner/201110/why-are-dogs-so-frequently-called-fido.

Greenwood, Arin. "Abraham Lincoln Obsessed Over His Dog Just Like You Do." *Huffington Post*, updated December 7, 2017. https://www.huffingtonpost.com.au/2015/04/14/abraham-lincoln-dog-animal-lover_n_7055640.html.

America's First Animal Shelters
Bershadker, Matt. "Telling the Full Story of America's Animal Shelters." ASPCA blog. https://www.aspca.org/.

Cronin, Keri. "Her Convictions Were Positive": The Legacy of Caroline Earle White." Unbound Project, October 13, 2016. https://unboundproject.org/caroline-earle-white/.

Hecht, Julie. "The History of Science in Animal Shelters." *Dog Spies* (blog), *Scientific American*, April 30, 2016. https://blogs.scientificamerican.com/dog-spies/the-history-of-science-in-animal-shelters/.

Alexander Graham Bell's Dog
Gallaudet, Edward Miner. "The Milan Convention." *American Annals of the Deaf* 26 (January 1881): 1–16. http://saveourdeafschools.org/edward_miner_gallaudet_the_milan_convention.pdf.

Messenger, Stephen. "Before Inventing the Telephone, Alexander Graham Bell Tried to Teach His Dog to Talk." The Dodo, March 29, 2014. https://www.thedodo.com/before-inventing-the-telephone-489117573.html.

Rosenwald, Michael S. "Your iPhone's Secret Past: How Cadaver Ears and a Talking Dog Led to the Telephone." *The Washington Post*, November 3, 2017. https://www.washingtonpost.com/news/retropolis/wp/2017/11/03/how-alexander-graham-bells-talking-dog-led-to-the-iphone-x/?utm_term=.9687992cbecf.

Bud Nelson
Adrea (username). "Bud Nelson Ready to Ride: First Dog to Drive Cross-Country." Life with Dogs, November 6, 2016. https://www.lifewithdogs.tv/2016/11/bud-nelson-ready-to-ride-first-dog-to-drive-cross-country/.

"Bud—the first dog to Travel Across United States by Automobile." Wolfstoria, September 11, 2015. https://www.wolfstoria.com/discover-these-doggies/bud-the-first-dog-to-travel-across-united-states-by-automobile/.

"The First Dog to Drive Across America." National Purebred Dog Day, July 23, 2016. https://nationalpurebreddogday.com/first-dog-to-drive-across-america/.

Lizzie Borden's Dogs
Hageman, William. "Lizzie Borden, Animal Lover." *Chicago Tribune*, September 30, 2014. https://www.chicagotribune.com/g00/lifestyles/pets/ct-pets-lizzie-0930-20141001-story.html?i10c.ua=1&i10c.encReferrer=aHR0cHM6Ly93d3cuZ-29vZ2xlLmNvbS8%3d&i10c.dv=2.

"Lizzie Borden and the Animal Rescue League of Fall River." The Animal Rescue League of Fall River, n.d. http://arlfr.com/lizzie-borden-and-arlfr.

Stickeen

Editors of *Encyclopaedia Brittanica.* "John Muir: Scottish-Born American Naturalist." *Encyclopaedia Brittanica*, updated April 17, 2019. https://www.britannica.com/biography/John-Muir.

Stickeen: The Story of a Dog by John Muir." EasyPetMD, n.d. http://www.easypetmd.com/doginfo/stickeen-story-dog-john-muir.

Dog Movie Stars

Chalakoski, Martin. "Terry, the Ultra-professional Canine Actor Who Played Toto, Earned More Than Most of *The Wizard of Oz* cast." https://www.thevintagenews.com/2017/12/01/toto-the-wizard-of-oz/.

"Hollywood Walk of Fame Honors Lassie, Rin Tin Tin, Strongheart . . . but Not Asta. A Travesty, We Say!" *L.A. Unleashed* (blog), *Los Angeles Times*, March 9, 2010. https://latimesblogs.latimes.com/unleashed/2010/03/hollywood-walk-of-fame-dogs-lassie-rin-tin-tin-strongheart-but-no-asta.html.

Orlean, Susan. "Rin Tin Tin: The Dog Who Charmed the World." *The Telegraph*, January 15, 2012. https://www.telegraph.co.uk/culture/books/9010387/Rin-Tin-Tin-the-dog-who-charmed-the-world.html.

Titanic **Dogs**

Arnold, Brandy. "Remembering the Dogs of the *Titanic*." *The Dogington Post*, April 12, 2019. https://www.dogingtonpost.com/dogs-on-the-titanic/.

Lou, JoAnna. "Dogs of the *Titanic*: The Doomed Ship's Survivors Included Three Canines." *Bark*, updated July 2016. https://thebark.com/content/dogs-titanic.

Wilson, Andrew. "Why the *Titanic* Still Fascinates Us." *Smithsonian Magazine*, March 2012. https://www.smithsonianmag.com/history/why-the-titanic-still-fascinates-us-98137822/.

Therapy Dogs

Albrecht, Brian. "Smoky of World War II Recognized by U.S. War Dogs Association." *The Plain Dealer* (Cleveland), October 13, 2017. https://www.cleveland.com/metro/2017/10/smoky_of_world_war_ii_recogniz.html.

"A History of Animal-Assisted Therapy." Alliance of Therapy Dogs, July 11, 2018. https://www.therapydogs.com/animal-therapy/.

Pellegrini, Ann. "The Dogs of War and the Dogs at Home: Thresholds of Loss." *American Imago* 66, no. 2 (Summer 2009): 231–51. https://www.jstor.org/stable/26305498?seq=1#page_scan_tab_contents.

Dogs of World War I

"Cigarette Dogs: Delivering Free Smokes." Famous Dogs in History, May 19, 2016. http://dogs-in-history.blogspot.com/2016/05/cigarette-dogs-delivering-free-smokes.html.

Cole, Linda. "Satan: The WWI Canine Hero Who Saved Lives at Verdun." Canidae.com, November 10, 2017. https://www.canidae.com/blog/2017/11/satan-the-wwi-canine-hero-who-saved-lives-at-verdun/.

"The Great War: 1914–1918." K-9 History, n.d. https://www.k9history.com/the-great-war-1914-1918.htm.

Joy and the Romanovs

Azar, Helen. "Romanov Family Pets." The Romanov Family, August 10, 2015. https://www.theromanovfamily.com/the-romanov-family-pets/.

Baklitskaya, Kate. "Royal Dog Fled from Siberia into British Exile, Living in Shadow of Windsor Castle." *The Siberian Times*, January 21, 2014. http://siberiantimes.com/other/others/features/royal-dog-fled-from-siberia-into-british-exile-living-in-shadow-of-windsor-castle/.

Thornhill, Ted. "Great Escape of the Royal Spaniel: Remarkable Story of How the Last Tsar of Russia's Dog Dodged Bullets as His Master Was Slaughtered by a Bolshevik Murder Squad . . . and Ended Up Living in Windsor." *Daily Mail*, January 27, 2014. https://www.dailymail.co.uk/news/article-2546612/Miracle-survival-Joy-spaniel-escaped-Bolshevik-murder-squad.html.

War of the Stray Dog

"Roll Over and Play Dead—The Ridiculous War of the Stray Dog." Military History Now, September 7, 2012. https://militaryhistorynow.com/2012/09/07/roll-over-and-play-dead-the-ridiculous-war-of-the-stray-dog/.
"The War of the Stray Dog: How Far Would You Go for Your Pet?" Ridiculous History, March 5, 2019. https://ridiculoushistoryshow.com/podcasts/the-war-of-the-stray-dog-how-far-would-you-go-for-your-pet.htm.

The Race of Mercy

"The Great Race of Mercy." The History of Vaccines, https://www.historyofvaccines.org/content/great-race-mercy.

"Iditarod: Celebrating the 'Great Race of Mercy' to Stop Diphtheria Outbreak in Alaska." CDC 24-7, Centers for Disease Control and Prevention, n.d. https://www.cdc.gov/about/24-7/savinglives/diphtheria/index.html.

The Royal Corgis

Doyle, Mika. "The Queen's Dorgis Are the Corgi Mix You Probably Never Knew Existed." Bustle, October 26, 2018. https://www.bustle.com/p/the-queens-dorgis-are-the-corgi-mix-you-probably-never-knew-existed-13005179.

Gold, Michael. "8 Decades of British Royal Corgis Reportedly at an End." *The New York Times*, April 18, 2018. https://www.nytimes.com/2018/04/18/world/europe/corgi-dogs-queen-elizabeth.html.

Nelson, Brooke. "The Real Reason Queen Elizabeth II Has Owned So Many Corgis." *Reader's Digest*, n.d. https://www.rd.com/culture/queen-elizabeth-corgis/.

Buddy, the First Seeing-Eye Dog

The Seeing Eye. https://www.seeingeye.org/.

Shea, Erin. "7 Things You Probably Didn't Know About Guide Dogs." American Kennel Club, October 28, 2016. https://www.akc.org/expert-advice/lifestyle/7-things-you-probably-didnt-know-about-guide-dogs/.

The Hoover Dam Dog

Anthony, Mark. "Remembering Nig, the Hoover Dam Dog." The Vegas Tourist, February 21, 2019. https://www.thevegastourist.com/blog/remembering-nig-the-hoover-dam-dog/.

"The Dog Who 'Owned' Hoover Dam." *RalieTravels* (blog), May 8, 2016. https://ralietravels.wordpress.com/2016/05/08/the-dog-who-owned-hoover-dam/.
"The Hoover Dam Dog: A Story." *Vivienne's Travel, Cultural, & Life Musings* (blog), n.d. http://www.viviennemackie.com/USAarticles/Hoover_Dam_Dog.html.

Hitler's Talking Dog Army

Daugherty, Greg. "When Don the Talking Dog Took the Nation by Storm." *Smithsonian Magazine*, April 23, 2018. https://www.smithsonianmag.com/history/when-don-talking-dog-took-nation-storm-180968867/.

"Nazis Tried to Train Dogs to Talk, Read and Spell to Win WW2." *The Telegraph*, May 24, 2011. https://www.telegraph.co.uk/news/newstopics/howaboutthat/8532573/Nazis-tried-to-train-dogs-to-talk-read-and-spell-to-win-WW2.html.

Robot and the Lascaux Cave Paintings
Charj, Charles. "Remembering Robot, the Dog Who Discovered a Trove of Prehistoric Art." Dogster, July 6, 2012. https://www.dogster.com/lifestyle/robot-the-dog.

Groeneveld, Emma. "Lascaux Cave." *Ancient History Encyclopedia*, September 6, 2016. https://www.ancient.eu/Lascaux_Cave/.

"The Myth Lascaux." Lascaux IV: International Centre for Cave Art, n.d. https://www.lascaux.fr/en/contenu/36-the-myth-lascaux.

World War II Dogs
Backovic, Lazar. "Britain's Luftwoofe: The Heroic Paradogs of World War II." *Spiegel Online*, December 17, 2013. https://www.spiegel.de/international/zeitgeist/the-parachuting-dogs-of-the-british-army-in-world-war-ii-a-939002.html.

Johnson, Daniel. "'Paradogs' Lured with Meat Out of Aircraft Behind Enemy Lines in WWII." *The Telegraph*, May 3, 2019. https://www.telegraph.co.uk/history/world-war-two/10211307/Paradogs-lured-with-meat-out-of-aircraft-behind-enemy-lines-in-WWII.html.

Paltzer, Seth. "The Dogs of War: The U.S. Army's Use of Canines in WWII." National Museum of the U.S. Army, June 2, 2016. https://armyhistory.org/the-dogs-of-war-the-u-s-armys-use-of-canines-in-wwii/.

Laika and Dogs in Space
Beischer, DE, and Fregly, AR. "Animals and Man in Space. A Chronology and Annotated Bibliography Through the Year 1960." Rubicon Foundation, 1962. http://archive.rubicon-foundation.org/xmlui/handle/123456789/9288.

Perritano, John. "10 Dogs Who Made History." How Stuff Works, March 17, 2018. https://animals.howstuffworks.com/pets/10-dogs-who-made-history2.htm.

"Russian Dogs Lost in Space." Space Today Online, n.d. http://www.spacetoday.org/Astronauts/Animals/Dogs.html.

Martha and the Beatles
"Paul McCartney's Dog Martha Is Born." History.com, A&E Networks, n.d. https://www.history.co.uk/this-day-in-history/16-june/paul-mccartneys-dog-martha-is-born.

"Wild Things: 11 Pets That Influenced Rock and Pop." *Rolling Stone*, May 2, 2014. https://www.rollingstone.com/music/music-lists/wild-things-11-pets-that-influenced-rock-and-pop-19600/.

Gompo
"Biography of Nelson Mandela." Nelson Mandela Foundation. https://www.nelsonmandela.org/content/page/biography.

Gable, Dawn. "Nelson Mandela's Afro-Cuban Dog." *Havana Times*, July 20, 2012. https://havanatimes.org/?p=74709.

Launder, Mimi. "13 Things You Should Know About Nelson Mandela." *Indy100* (blog), *The Independent*, July 18, 2018. https://www.indy100.com/article/nelson-mandela-birthday-anniversary-centenary-apartheid-8451571.

The Canine Rescue Teams of 9/11
AKC Staff. "Meet the 9/11 Dogs: Roselle, Who Helped Her Blind Partner Escape the WTC." American Kennel Club, September 11, 2015. https://www.akc.org/expert-advice/news/meet-the-9-11-dogs-roselle-who-helped-her-blind-partner-escape-the-wtc/.

Edwards, Anna. "The 9/11 Rescue Dogs: Portraits of the Last Surviving Animals Who Scoured Ground Zero One Decade On." *Daily Mail*, September 5, 2011. https://www.dailymail.co.uk/news/article-2033628/Surviving-9-11-rescue-dogs-scoured-Ground-Zero-bodies-commemorated-decade-difficult-mission.html.

"Remembering the Four-Legged Heroes of the 9/11 Rescue and Recovery." 9/11 Memorial & Museum, May 24, 2017. https://www.911memorial.org/blog/remembering-four-legged-heroes-911-rescue-and-recovery.

Snuppy
Hess, Peter. "Scientists Make Even More Clones of Snuppy, the First Cloned Dog." *Inverse*, November 21, 2017. https://www.inverse.com/article/38620-snuppy-dog-clone-afghan-hound-seoul-dolly.

Latson, Jennifer. "What Happened to the First Cloned Puppy." *Time*, April 24, 2015. http://time.com/3822573/snuppy/.

Osborne, Hannah. "World's First Cloned Dog Used to Make More Cloned Dogs so Scientists Can See What Happens." *Newsweek*, November 23, 2017. https://www.newsweek.com/dogs-cloned-snuppy-worlds-first-cloned-dog-720725.

Rupee
Grossman, Samantha. "Meet the First Dog to Climb Mt. Everest (Spoiler: He's Adorable)." *TimeNewsfeed* (blog), *Time*, November 12, 2013. http://newsfeed.time.com/2013/11/12/meet-the-first-dog-to-climb-mt-everest-hint-hes-adorable/.

Schmitz, Ashleigh. "Meet Rupee, the First Dog to Ever Climb Mt. Everest." *Parade*, November 13, 2013. https://parade.com/228971/ashleighschmitz/meet-rupee-the-first-dog-to-ever-climb-mt-everest/.

Extinct Dogs
Carlson, Tom. "These 21 Old Dog Breeds No Longer Exist Today . . . But You'll Wish They Were Still Around." Honest to Paws, n.d. http://honesttopaws.com/extinct-dogs-breeds/2/?as=538Steam&pas=113.

Clark, Mike. "What Are Bully Dog Breeds?" DogTime, n.d. https://dogtime.com/reference/60537-bully-dog-breeds.

"Hawaiian Poi Dog." Dog Breed Info. https://www.dogbreedinfo.com/hawaiianpoidog.htm.

"St. John's Water Dog." EasyPetMD. http://www.easypetmd.com/doginfo/st-johns-water-dog.

Shrumm, Regan. "Salish Woolly Dog." *The Canadian Encyclopedia*, updated February 11, 2019. https://www.thecanadianencyclopedia.ca/en/article/salish-woolly-dog.